# BRAIN
## GAMES
## FOR
## DOGS

# BRAIN

# GAMES
# FOR
# DOGS

## CLAIRE ARROWSMITH

### FIREFLY BOOKS

# A FIREFLY BOOK

Published by Firefly Books Ltd. 2011

Seventh printing, 2017

**Publisher Cataloging-in-Publication Data**

Arrowsmith, Claire.
    Brain games for dogs / Claire Arrowsmith.
[160] p. : col. photos. ; cm.
Includes bibliographical references.
Summary: A compendium of fun games, tricks
and activities that can be enjoyed with a dog to
stretch and challenge it mentally, and to allow it
to enjoy a quality workout for mind and body.
ISBN-13: 978-1-55407-490-7   (pbk.)
1. Dogs—Training. 2. Dogs—Psychology.
3. Dogs—Behavior. I. Title.
636.70887 dc22   SF431.A7769 2010

**Library and Archives Canada Cataloguing in
Publication**

Arrowsmith, Claire
    Brain games for dogs / Claire Arrowsmith.
Includes bibliographical references.
ISBN 978-1-55407-490-7
    1. Games for dogs. 2. Dogs—Training. I. Title.
SF427.45.A77 2010   636.7'0887   C2010-900572-4

Published in the United States by
Firefly Books (U.S.) Inc.
P.O. Box 1338, Ellicott Station
Buffalo, New York 14205

Published in Canada by
Firefly Books Ltd.
50 Staples Ave, Unit 1
Richmond Hill, Ontario L4B 0A7

Printed in Singapore

**Disclaimer**
The information and recommendations in
this book are given without any guarantees
on behalf of the author and publisher, who
disclaim any liability with the use of this material.

**Author's Note**
Brain games are intended to be played by all
dogs but I have chosen to describe participating
dogs as male throughout the descriptions that
will found in the book. This is purely to simplify
the text and does not mean to imply that any or
all of the games are not suitable for female dogs.

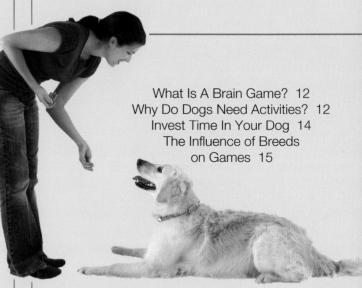

What Is A Brain Game?  12
Why Do Dogs Need Activities?  12
Invest Time In Your Dog  14
The Influence of Breeds
on Games  15

Chapter **TWO**

# The Basic Skills

Why Use Positive Training Methods?  26
Rules Of Game Play  26
Using Rewards In Play  28
Using Food As Rewards  29
What Treats?  31
Your Dog Can Win Jackpots!  32
Reducing The Rewards  33
What Motivates Your Dog?  34
Where To Begin Brain Games?  35
When To Begin Brain Games?  36
Have Realistic Aims  36
Take A Break  38
Why Good Ground Rules Are Important  38
Should You Try Clicker Training?  39
Getting Your Timing Right  40
Getting Started With A Clicker  42

# CONTENTS

## PART 1: PREPARE TO PLAY BRAIN GAMES 8

### Chapter ONE

## Introducing Brain Games

Examples of Breed Type and General Play Preference  18
The Influence of Age on Play  19
Why Health Is Important In Brain Games  20
Which Games To Play?  22
Playing With Multiple Pets  23
Behavior Problems  24
Brain Games
Guidelines  25

Training Without A Clicker  42
Shaping Behaviors To Build A Game  43
Brain Games Involving Toys  43
Safety Considerations:
The Size, Shape And
Structure Of Toys 44
Other Injury Risks  46
Teaching Basic Play
Skills To Timid Or
New Dogs 47
Rescued Dogs  48

Avoiding Problems
and Resolving
Minor Issues 49
Charting Your
Progress  51
Using Hand Signals  52
Introducing Verbal
Cues  53
Minimizing Cues  55
Coping When Training Doesn't Go
As Planned  56
Avoid Punishment During Games  56
Being Prepared To Play  57

**CONTENTS continued overleaf** ▶

# PART 2: LET THE BRAIN GAMES BEGIN 58

Chapter **THREE**

## It's Puppy-Play

Puppy Chew Chew  60
Puppy Retrieve  62
Go To Bed  64
Take It and Leave It  66

Chapter **FOUR**

## Games At Home

Activity Toys and Boredom Busters  68
Find It!  74
The Leg Weave  74
Jump Over  76
Limbo Dancing  76
Doorbell Dash  78
Where Are My Keys?  80
The Canine Cleaner  82
Tidy Your Toys  83

Chapter **FIVE**

## Games For Small Areas

Foot Touch  88
Push The Door Closed  88
Indoor Agility  90
Play Box  90

Chapter **SIX**

## Games For The Garden

Digging For Treasure  92
Frozen Popsicles  92
Toy Bungee  94
Skipping  94

Creating An Outdoor Obstacle Course  96
Jumping Hoops  96
Tunnel Dash  98
Zigzagging  98

Chapter **SEVEN**

## Games To Play While Out And About

Extendable Excitement  100
Skater Dog  102
Hide and Seek  104
Carry It  104
Nature's Obstacle Course  106
Egg And Spoon Race 106

Chapter **EIGHT**

## Verbal Games

Multilingual Tricks  108
Toy Identity Parade  110

Chapter **NINE**

## Traveling Games

Catch The Treat  112
In-Car Entertainment  113
Poker Face  114

Chapter **TEN**

## Water Games

Bobbing For Treats  116
Dunking and Diving  118
The Great Water Race  118

Chapter **ELEVEN**

# Games For Less Active Dogs

Balance A Treat On Your Paw  120
Balance A Treat On Your Nose  122
Shy Dog  122

Chapter **TWELVE**

# Search Games

Fastest Canine Eye  124
Out Of Sight But Not Out Of Mind  126
Go Get... 128

Chapter **THIRTEEN**

# Armchair Games

Reach Out And Touch  130
How Do You Do?  130
Hop Over  132
Sneeze and Retrieve!  134
Say Your Prayers  134
Fetch The Bowl  136
Changing Channels  138

Chapter **FOURTEEN**

# Games for Specific Breeds

Terriers  140
Scenthounds  141
Herding Dogs  142
Sighthounds  143

Chapter **FIFTEEN**

# Party Games

Shake A Paw  144
Waving Hi and
  Goodbye  146
Spinning Around
  and Around  148
Rollin' Rover  150
Playing Dead  152
Crawling Canine  152
Bedtime!  154
Multiple Dog Party Tricks  155

Chapter **SIXTEEN**

# Competitive Games

Agility  156
Flyball  156
Frisbee, Flying Disc or Disc Dog  157
Obedience  157
Heelwork to Music or Canine Freestyle  157
Earthdog Trials  157
Lure Coursing  158
Dock Diving or Splash Dogs  158
Tracking  158
CaniX  158
Sledding  158
Field Trials  159
Herding Trials  159
Rally-Obedience  159

Acknowledgments  160
Picture Credits  160

# PREPARE

# PART ONE

# TO PLAY BRAIN GAMES

# INTRODUCING BRAIN GAMES

The fact that you are reading about *Brain Games* for your dog means that you have an interest in keeping him or her active and happy. Some people will be looking for ways to encourage their dog to be more active, some will want suggestions to occupy their dog while they are away, while others may just want some ideas to put the fun back into playing with their pet. Even with the best of intentions we often get stuck in a rut playing the same old games with our dogs. And even these may diminish over time as we lose interest in following the same old routine.

Many owners will claim that their dog does enjoy playing but, when pressed, they can only list one or two games that he plays. One favorite game may be useful for training or for keeping the dog occupied, but generally it is not sufficient and the dog is left under-stimulated or over-focused on one activity which in itself can lead to problems.

We love our dogs deeply and view them, quite rightly, as highly intelligent animals. The truly wonderful thing is that dogs actually do love learning and discovering new ways to fill their days, to use up their abundant energy and to interact with the humans in their pack. This gives us lots of scope to work and play with our dogs. In fact, our imagination is the only limiting factor regarding the number of things that we can do together.

## KEEP TOPPING UP YOUR TRAINING

Many people will teach their dog the basic commands and then declare him "trained." Whatever the owner may say, the dog's learning and development will continue whether his owner is making time for him or not. He will still require stimulation, activity and fun. When I meet owners of young dogs who declare after a short puppy training course that their dog has finished its training, I often think how frustrating it would be for us if our education ended when we were still in childhood. If we had to

**LEFT** With a bit of ingenuity you can find all sorts of new opportunities for play around the house — but take care with balls near stairways.

**ABOVE** Games in the open air with an energetic dog are times when you can both have fun and strengthen your relationship.

**ABOVE** It's quite surprising what skills a dog can master when you let your imagination really take flight!

keep on repeating the same lessons over and over again, we would all soon get bored and lack enthusiasm. Think about how many limitations that would put on your lifestyle and your ability to interact appropriately and cope in this world.

It is just as important that a dog's education continues, especially since an untrained or frustrated dog can be dangerous. This is why it is critical that all dog owners think carefully about their dog's routine and lifestyle and take the time to make provision for new games. The benefits are enormous as a contented, stimulated dog is less likely to develop many of the more common behavioral problems. This makes pet ownership much easier overall.

The more time you spend having fun training and playing with your pet, the stronger the bond between you will be.

Friendship grows from the fun you have together and vital trust can then form. A strong relationship between a dog and his owner is special and highly rewarding.

**BELOW** Happy dog, happy owner. Enjoyable playtime often leads to a greater degree of mutual trust.

**LEFT** A dog left alone inside the home for long periods will inevitably lack stimulation.

Many dogs lack sufficient stimulation during their normal daily life because their days are spent completely within their home environment. This can become very predictable and, to put a human term to the emotion, boring. This means that these dogs are not living a fulfilled existence. Dogs that have not had the chance to use up their energy are likely to become over-excitable and difficult to handle, making any sort of obedience training difficult. Even periods of play with these dogs dwindle because they become too excited when you do try to play and can't learn the concept of even simple games like "Fetch." Lack of stimulation is thus a contributing factor to many behavioral complaints. These can vary from behaviors that are inconvenient and annoying; such as some destructive habits or barking, to problems which are much more distressing and dangerous, such as self-mutilation or frustration-related aggression.

# WHAT IS A BRAIN GAME?

A *brain game* is any activity that provides your dog with mental stimulation. It fulfills your dog's needs for entertainment and provides a challenge which is stimulating and exciting. Some brain games also provide physical stimulation which is equally as important for the overall well-being of your dog. Some activities require you to spend time training your dog, while others will provide your dog with an activity to enjoy while you are out or will be pursued just for the fun of it.

# WHY DO DOGS NEED ACTIVITIES?

In the wild, your dog would have had to work alongside his pack or by himself to track down potential prey using his olfactory (scent) ability, his hearing and his vision. He would then stalk, chase and catch the prey, or even dig it out of the ground. Dead prey would then need to be dismantled to access the most nutritious parts. On top of this, he would spend time exploring his environment, interacting with his fellow pack members, mating and warding off intruders. Females also had the job of bringing up their pups.

**LEFT** Boredom and frustration can lead to antisocial behavior, such as persistent barking.

**LEFT** Without stimulation, a domestic dog can lead a one-dimensional life. Such dogs are harder to train because they may become over-excited when they do receive attention.

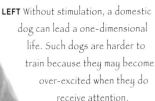

**RIGHT** An activity toy can keep a dog occupied and contented on his own when guests come to call.

could be to you on a daily basis. For example, if you own an enthusiastic dog who loves to greet your guests and doesn't easily settle down, giving him another task or game to play will help to redirect his attention and relieve your guests who may not all share your adoration for your dog.

Although your dog is lucky enough to live with you as a companion animal, he still has a natural inclination to use his senses, expend energy and to process new information. A sedentary life within the home can result in a dog that feels stressed and frustrated. Luckily, it is easy to introduce new activities to keep dogs of all shapes, sizes, ages and temperaments feeling fulfilled and happy.

Behaviorists and trainers will tell you that a dog engaged in a good brain game is typically one that is not getting himself into trouble. This can be extremely useful to all owners. Consider how beneficial this

**BELOW** A good brain game adds a bit of sparkle to life and keeps your dog alert and eager for more.

Other dogs that have highly exuberant characteristics are often more difficult to control and owners frequently ask for techniques to calm their dog. There are many tips that will help and brain games are critical aids. Don't expect to achieve calm behavior overnight if your dog's natural temperament is to be high-spirited.

However, by teaching your dog new ways to use up his energy and by training him to follow a number of clear commands, you will find that he will focus more easily and gets less frustrated.

**LEFT** This game encourages a dog to forage for a treat that is hidden inside a container with a spinning top. It's good for a dog left on his own.

problem can be diverted by introducing some clever, well-timed activities.

If your dog is chewing up your home, stealing from counters or leaping up at visitors, then the chances are that he needs to be given some more appropriate activities to keep him out of trouble. So, *Brain Games* isn't just about you having fun together, it has a sound practical grounding in training.

## INVEST TIME IN YOUR DOG

Pet dogs deserve our time and attention. Remember that not finding time to teach

**LEFT** Naturally high-spirited, energetic dogs need to let off steam, both physically and mentally. A brain game can be just the job to keep him focused on his owner.

**BELOW** Some dogs develop destructive habits around the home for the want of something better to keep them occupied.

Having a fun, reliable game to play that your dog is confident with can even help to keep more worried dogs in a positive emotional state when they are around things that they find unfamiliar and scary. While a game won't prevent a full-blown phobic response, a developing sensitivity

**RIGHT** Different breeds of dog have different abilities and characteristics. Try to take account of this in your choice of games.

your dog new games will not stop him from learning new things; it will just make it more likely that he will learn inappropriate activities, such as barking, jumping up or perhaps digging up your flowers. Resolving these issues or replacing destroyed possessions takes time and money. Playing games is much more fun and easier on both your stress-levels and on your bank balance.

## THE INFLUENCE OF BREEDS ON GAMES

Obviously there is great variation in the types of games that dogs like to play. Indeed it is important to be aware that different breeds will lean towards different types of games and styles of play. Different breeds arose because humans identified dogs that were good at doing particular jobs and bred them with other dogs that had similar skills. These abilities were passed on through the dog's genes and, over time, their offspring became better and better at the task they were being bred to do. In the same way humans have created dogs that have a particular physical appearance — by breeding two long-legged dogs together, for instance, there is a good chance that the offspring that result from their mating will also have longer legs.

**ABOVE** Your dog's ancestry is part of his character. Cocker Spaniels, for instance, were bred to find, flush out and retrieve gamebirds. By understanding this side of his nature you can engage his instincts in appropriate activities.

15

We have selected dogs with different skills and created all the breeds that we see today, as well as many that no longer exist. Early dogs were bred with a particular function in mind and over time we created dogs that were extremely highly motivated to perform that function. There were dogs bred to perform almost all imaginable jobs in order to help their human owners.

Nowadays, most of the approximately 200 known breeds are simply kept as household pets without having a real job assigned to them, but their inherited desire to perform certain behaviors will still be present to some extent. Mixed breed dogs will also have inherited tendencies which need satisfying.

*The Whippet is a highly functional worker who retains his hunting instinct.*

# BREED GROUPS

| Toys | This variable group of dogs consists of small dogs which are now kept as companion pets. However, the | origins of many breeds can be traced back to larger versions with working origins. |
|------|-------------------------------------------------------------------------------------------------------|-------------------------------------------------------------------------------------|
| **Hounds** | The purpose of this group was to help man locate and chase down prey animals. Shapes and sizes varied depending on the habitat | they were working in. Some have excellent sight or scenting ability while others have exceptional speed or endurance. |
| **Pastoral** | This new group consists of various dogs originally included as "working dogs." This group all originally worked with flocks, herding and | often guarding livestock against various predators. These tend to be intelligent, active dogs with high stamina. |
| **Terriers** | Most of the dogs in this group were bred to hunt vermin and they often have a willingness to go to ground. | These breeds are brave and tenacious. They have fast reactions and are often independent. |
| **Utility Dogs** | This group includes dogs that don't comfortably fit in other groups and the breeds included vary between countries. Many had purposes that | are no longer required today and so they vary between hunting, fighting, high stamina carriage dogs and even guarding breeds. |

The versatile Lab is a gundog as well as a loving companion.

| | | |
|---|---|---|
| **Gundogs or Sporting Dogs** | These were designed to help find game and retrieve the prey once shot. Depending on the breed, they would either point out the animal | or help to flush them out. Some will then readily retrieve the shot game. Some were especially bred to work in and around water. |
| **Working Dogs** | These dogs tend to be strong and hardy and many still work today. Purposes vary and include | guarding, hunting, fighting, tracking, sledding, cattle driving and those used as watchdogs. |
| **Other Miscellaneous** | There are many other breeds that are not consistently classified into the above categories, often due to their specific distribution in one country or region. Understanding the nature of these breeds will require you to research the breed's | history and original purpose. Crossed breeds, mongrels and new breed types also have their own temperament and instincts. Find out as much about your own particular dog as you can. |

**ABOVE** Huskies are working dogs that love to run. Teams of dogs are well suited to sled-racing where their energy and light-footedness can be profitably harnessed.

The job a dog has been bred for will influence the activities in which he prefers to engage, including the types of games that he will play. Get to know your own dog's breed and history. Researching and reading about the history of a breed will develop your understanding of the differences between dogs. It is not just a dog's shape and looks that differ; its instincts and desires are just as variable.

# EXAMPLES OF BREED TYPE AND GENERAL PLAY PREFERENCES

**ABOVE** Typically terrier — a Jack Russell going to ground.

**ABOVE** Newfoundlands were bred to haul fishing nets in water.

**ABOVE** Border Collies are natural herding animals.

**Jack Russell Terriers** often love to dig, burrow into tunnels and usually become excited about squeaky toys.

**Cocker Spaniels** love playing scent games and "find it" challenges just as they would in the field.

**Newfoundlands** have a strong desire to get into water and will happily dive in whenever the opportunity arises.

**Border Collies** are stimulated by movement and like to try to round up the animals and people in their presence. They often love chasing balls and Frisbees but can direct their focus into excelling in many canine sporting activities due to their physical ability and fast responses.

**Mixed breed dogs** will inherit characteristics from their parents and are likely to exhibit various characteristics from both sides. If you don't know what your dog's parentage was, you can gain some idea from looking at his physical shape and size as well as by considering his temperament. Experiment with different activities and always make sure that your dog is physically able to manage the game.

Whatever kind of dog you have, he will benefit from brain games to provide mental and physical stimulation. However, if your dog was originally bred to do a job

Puppies typically enjoy chewing.

**LEFT** You can start to introduce even young puppies to interactive games by getting them interested in a squeaky ball.

he will be especially thrilled to have a new activity to take part in. While all dogs are in need of some brain games, those probably in greatest need are young puppies, adolescents and those from active working backgrounds.

## THE INFLUENCE OF AGE ON PLAY

**Puppies** It may be surprising to learn that even very tiny puppies at just three weeks are already beginning to show signs of play behavior. When the puppy is very young, he initially just tries simple pawing which then develops into jumping, chasing and wrestling. They will also play with toys placed near them and this is a perfect opportunity to begin interactive games.

Young dogs can be taught to seek out toys when they feel like playing. If they don't get the opportunity to play with their own toys, they are more likely to focus their attention on

household items, family members or other pets. With some breeds if you neglect to introduce toys while they are young, it becomes very difficult to encourage toy-play later on in life. This includes many of the hound breeds.

Teething will influence your young dog's desire to chew on toys. This occurs when your puppy loses his milk teeth and then later in adolescence when the adult teeth are growing in the jaw. During this time your dog will need to be given appropriate things to chew and mouth on. A sore mouth may put your puppy off playing so choose appropriate items.

**BELOW** Littermates enjoy pawing at one another from a young age. This develops into jumping and wrestling games that teach the pup about the dynamics of social interaction.

While they are young, dogs should not be encouraged to jump or behave exuberantly (they'll probably do enough of this by themselves without any enticement). Wait until your dog has physically matured to avoid any risk to his growing limbs and joints. The larger breeds are more at risk from this type of damage. If in doubt, always seek advice from your vet and be sensible.

**Elderly Dogs** As dogs age they experience physical changes which affect their sight, hearing and taste. These senses begin to deteriorate and this will influence their ability to play by making it harder to detect scents, spot movements and to hear commands. They will also begin to feel the signs of aging in their joints and limbs which will limit their ability to physically move around. Of course, exercise is good for the body and overall longevity and so a dog that has been used to activity throughout its life will probably cope better with a new activity than an unfit, elderly dog.

Although a dog's early experience of

**LEFT** Avoid energetic jumping games until your dog has physically matured and his joints and limbs are robust enough to cope.

playing will influence his later ability to respond to toys and humans, all dogs can be taught to perform new actions and to respond to new signals throughout their lives. Success may take longer with an elderly dog and the game you choose may be different, but it should be possible to introduce more games into your lives, no matter what age your dog is.

## WHY HEALTH IS IMPORTANT IN BRAIN GAMES

Just as in humans, the health of our dogs influences how active they are, how physically able they are and how willing they are to play. Before starting any new activity with your dog, you should assess what the physical demands of the game are. Before we humans begin a new gym program we are advised to have a health check and to discuss the requirements with our doctor. A dog can

**RIGHT** Even old dogs can learn new tricks! Don't stop playing games because your dog is aging.

be given a similar check-up by your veterinarian who will then advise you of any potential problems and also on a good feeding regime that suits your pet.

Illness may reduce appetite which in turn reduces the dog's motivation to earn treats. Your dog may not be physically able to jump or move in specific ways if he has skeletal or muscular problems. Hearing problems can make it much harder to hear commands or words of praise while poor eyesight or eye infections can make it difficult for your dog to see your signals or your equipment.

You should regularly check your dog over from head to toe so that you are

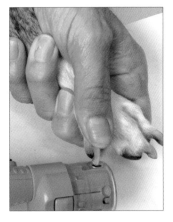

**LEFT** Overlong nails can be an impediment to a dog and unbalance his way of standing and running. Keep nails short by using clippers or an electric grinder like this.

**ABOVE** Ears should be regularly cleaned of wax and dirt, particularly if you own a breed with long, pendulous ears.

**BELOW** If you have any concerns about the overall health and fitness of your dog, it makes sense to have him checked by a vet before introducing a new regime of brain games.

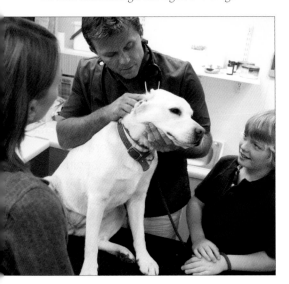

aware of any changes on his body. You can do this while you groom or bathe him as this will familiarize you with his normal body condition while letting you spot new lumps, bumps or scratches as soon as they appear. Your dog's nails need to be kept at an appropriate length and eyes and ears should be kept clean and free from excess hair. A build up of wax in the ears may indicate an infection but can also be the direct cause of hearing problems. Regular health check-ups will keep you aware of any problems that may be affecting your dog.

**RIGHT** Take care initially with dogs that are obese or naturally heavily built. Fitness will come over time.

personality traits will also tell you whether he prefers to work closely with you or can cope while working at a distance away from you. A dog that is only relaxed when he's close to you may find some of the distance tasks trickier.

Obesity is a major problem in pet dogs these days. While playing games with your dog is a great way to help him to lose weight by increasing his activity levels and by making him earn his food rations, it is wise to begin slowly and build up to more strenuous games. If your dog becomes over-tired or hurts himself during a game, then he is less likely to be enthusiastic next time you try to begin the fun. Some

There are many "rules" about game play and almost all dog owners have been given advice for or against most activities. Some suggestions are made for valid reasons as

**BELOW** Games should be times that both of you find enjoyable. Try to select play activities that suit your dog's temperament and which you also find fun.

people worry about using food during training *(left)* or play time believing it will make their dog fat. This should not be the case if the food is used correctly. Using food in brain games is discussed in Chapter 2.

some activities are dangerous and the risks outweigh the benefits. Other games must be assessed depending upon the dog's temperament and the particular situation. For example, a dog that displays resource guarding behavior (i.e. the guarding of toys, food or bedding) may not be ideal for a tug-of-war game and a dog with arthritis or back problems should not be encouraged to jump or even roll over. You should carefully consider your dog's

## WHICH GAMES TO PLAY?

Choosing games is partly about selecting activities that you will enjoy, but it is also strongly dependent upon your dog's natural instincts. Understanding your dog's

**BELOW** Think about your dog's physical conformation and fitness levels. A roll-over is a marvelous trick to teach a dog but you will not get anywhere with a pet that has back problems and finds the movement uncomfortable.

# PLAYING WITH MULTIPLE PETS

Owning more than one dog will also add to the complication of brain games. There will often be a degree of competition between the pets, which is natural. However, if your dogs compete to the point of aggression then you should be very cautious about introducing games involving objects or foods that are highly valued by them.

behavioral traits and health before choosing which games to play. These may vary over time as your dog goes through different life stages and degrees of health.

The games that you choose to introduce may also depend upon whether you have young children and how excitable your dog is. Always supervise play between dogs and children and make sure that you interrupt the game before either side becomes overly excited. Children may not know how to recognize when your dog is becoming too aroused or frustrated so it is the job of an adult to intervene and keep things safe.

**BELOW** If you want to play games with more than one dog, it's probably best to teach them individually first and then bring them together.

Dogs with equable temperaments who know one another well can make excellent playmates.

Noisy, excitable children and an inquisitive, impressionable young dog can create quite a volatile mixture.

**ABOVE** It's best if an adult supervises any game or training exercise involving young children and dogs.

Playing individual games is a better idea and can help you to ensure that your bond with each individual is strong while teaching them to cope with being away from one another. Carefully introducing activities with both dogs may be possible later on but it is better to have a helper present if you suspect problems.

**ABOVE** One ball, one hand, one dog — let's play a brain game.

items. Other problems include extreme nervousness, failure to return when let off the lead or perhaps over-boisterousness towards the owner. If your dog is behaving in a way that causes you concern, please ask your veterinarian to refer you to a qualified behaviorist to help you to resolve these issues before you start trying to learn new skills.

## CURRENT BEHAVIOR PROBLEMS

There are various behavioral problems that can cause difficulties when you are playing brain games. As already stated, if your dog responds in an aggressive way around food or toys, then you must address this problem before you play with the problem

## BRAIN GAMES GUIDELINES

Alongside the instructions for each brain game in this book you will see some additional information gathered in a table that will help you to choose appropriate games for you and your dog as well as making sure you're prepared with all the correct equipment.

ABOVE The guidelines included in the book will tell you which brain games are best played outdoors.

 = dog plays game alone

 = dog plays with his owner

 = dog plays game with more than one person

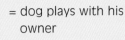 = group activity for several owners and their dogs

**Where?** This tells you about the location best suited for the game.

**What?** This is an indication of the items you'll need to play this game.

**Difficulty Level** To make it a little easier to know which games to try, each is given a star rating on a scale of 1–5: 1 Star = Beginner, 5 Star = Advanced. This is a guide only and some dogs are naturally going to pick up some games quicker than others depending on their breed instincts and body design. Indication is given if learning another game first will be useful.

**Interaction Level** Another quick indicator about the type of game is the Interaction Key telling you whether the game is suitable for solo play, or is more interactive. The key takes the following form:

BELOW You will enjoy a real sense of achievement when your dog starts to show you just how brainy he can be.

# THE BASIC SKILLS

The process of learning is complex and can be confusing. Understanding a few key points will allow you to think through your playing and training strategies logically, and so optimize your success and minimize failures.

**BELOW** Cooperation, not coercion, should be your watchword when training a dog.

into doing certain things if aversive techniques are used by their handler. However, this is not just unfair on the dog; it can also give rise to behavioral issues involving aggression or extreme fear. Brain games are intended to benefit both you and your dog and so it is important that you both actually enjoy them.

## RULES OF GAME PLAY

**1 Your dog will repeat any behavior that results in a pleasurable experience.** This can be the arrival of praise or a tasty treat during training. On the other hand, it may be unintentional, such as when a dog gets attention when

**ABOVE** When using treats, make sure you get your timing right so the dog is unambiguously rewarded for good behaviors.

## WHY USE POSITIVE TRAINING METHODS?

Positive training is essential for long-term good results and good relations. A harsh owner who punishes their dog's mistakes is likely to quash their dog's enthusiasm and end up with either a dog who dislikes training, or one that is less motivated to try out new behaviors next time. As pack animals, dogs can unfortunately be forced

he jumps up or eats a piece of toast stolen from the counter top. Make sure that your dog is rewarded only for the actions you like so he will begin to choose that option more often.

**2 Good timing is critical.** The longer you leave between the action and the giving of a reward, the less likely it is that your dog will make the desired association quickly. Imagine this scenario: your dog manages his first perfect roll-over. Instead of offering a reward immediately, you then go off to the kitchen in search of a treat. Your dog will get up out of the position, will move around and may have a sniff and a scratch, and then he walks across the room looking for you. He comes down the hallway where he sees the mail popping through the box and the kids running past him to play. He then enters the kitchen and stands by you at the cupboard where you are fighting to open a box of biscuits. By the time you offer him the treat, what do you think he will associate it with? How difficult must it be for a dog to understand that the biscuit was meant to encourage the roll-over he did before all the other events occurred. Scientific research has shown that the quicker the reward arrives, the faster an animal will learn. Ideally, this is within three seconds. Since this can be difficult when your dog is far away, or if you already have your hands full, verbal praise and clicker training (see pages 39–41) are useful to "mark" the correct response which you can then follow up with a treat.

**ABOVE** This scenario illustrates what can go wrong in a training regime. The dog has discovered the spilt food on the worktop and is hoovering it up. He has received a tasty reward for this behavior, but it is not one you want to encourage.

**BELOW** Follow up a good performance of a trick or game quickly with a reward.

**3 Punishment has problems.** Games are meant to be fun and there should not be any need to use punishment. The timing of punishment is arguably even more critical than for rewards. Unless the aversive experience occurs just as the dog is doing something wrong, it will have limited effect and he may become anxious. This will put an end to your games and could cause him to lose confidence in you.

**ABOVE** Most dogs will view play and the time spent interacting with you during a brain game as rewards in their own right.

**ABOVE** Use treats in training that your dog is going to value highly — he may view his daily kibble as just a bit boring.

**4 The payment is important.** You may feel that you want to use your dog's own kibble for training or a plain dog biscuit. While this will excite some dogs, for others these rewards are far less interesting than other things around them. Why should your dog work for another piece of kibble when he gets a bowl full of them twice a day for doing nothing? If your dog learns to associate a highly valued reward, such as a piece of meat, with an action, he is far more likely to want to try to earn it again later.

## USING REWARDS IN PLAY

Play itself is a rewarding experience so often extra incentive is not required. However, when your dog is learning any new task or skill, he may require some encouragement in the form of treats and definitely praise for getting it right. This will speed up the learning process and your dog will soon associate the new activity with the pleasure of the reward.

It has been shown time and time again in many situations that training using encouragement and rewards brings the most consistent and reliable results. This is why modern trainers and dog owners try to reward their dogs for performing in a desirable way. This can be for basic training, specialized obedience, tricks, or just nice

owner relationship is affected by using food. It's all about balance and ensuring that you have a good relationship with your dog in general. No one wants to own a dog that only sees them as a food dispenser. However, if your dog associates you with the arrival of the nice things in life, he will feel especially happy to see you and play with you. Using treats should not mean that you allow your dog to bully you into giving him treats when he likes. It is up to you to request an action which you can reward. Of course, there are also times when you want to reinforce a behavior that is occurring naturally (such as settling quietly) but that is your choice.

**ABOVE** Treats are available in many forms — it's up to you to discover which ones your dog values highly and to use them as rewards that you will choose for training purposes. But don't overdo it — a treat must remain a special bonus.

friendly behavior. Dogs that are brought up with positive training techniques tend to have more predictable responses and are more trusting towards people.

## USING FOOD AS REWARDS

You will probably be familiar with the concept of using treats in training. Those who don't use them usually have some misconceptions about training or how a dog-

**BELOW** Treats deftly maneuvered in front of a dog can be used to "shape" behaviors. You can lure a dog into a Sit or a Down with one, for instance.

**LEFT** Keep an eye on your dog's weight when using treat-based training. Obesity is to be avoided.

**BELOW RIGHT** Don't overfeed, like this. Measure out your dog's daily food allowance.

correctly, he will learn how you expect him to behave and then you can gradually reduce the amount of rewards offered. Of course, if you really get the training bug, then you may want to always have a few treats with you just in case your dog offers you an amazing action, or in case you get the urge to teach something new.

Occasional reinforcement of already established behaviors never does any harm and your dog will be delighted when he "wins" an unexpected prize.

Your dog should not only respond when you have a treat in your hand. If this occurs, the training has not been done properly or there are too many other distractions going on around the dog. It may also be that the food has simply been used to bribe the dog rather than to reward good behavior. In these cases it is best to go back to basics and advance through each stage again; making sure the appearance of the food and your timing is accurate.

A reward-based training program should not make your dog fat. Over-feeding with too little exercise will do this. If you are concerned about over-feeding, then you can measure out your dog's daily allowance in the morning and either use some of this food along with treats for training, or reduce the overall amount to compensate for the rewards the dog will earn that day. If your dog has had a busy training session, then he will not need a full bowl of food for his meal.

It's a popular misconception that you'll have to fill your pockets with treats forever more if you start training with food. This is not true. If you train your dog

Some dogs are not motivated by food while others have very sensitive digestions which mean they cannot be given tasty food. In these cases you may prefer to give them a toy when they get something right. However, using food is much easier and allows your training to progress much more quickly than if your dog is allowed

**LEFT** Some dogs are more motivated by a game with a toy than by a treat. So tailor your training methods to your dog's individual personality.

One hand directs the training, while the other sneaks into the pouch for a reward.

to go off playing with a toy after each success. Having said that, if your dog does a great retrieve or is happy to have a quick tuggy-tuggy game with you, then go ahead and use a toy.

## WHAT TREATS?

Tiny fingernail-sized pieces of food are great for training. Variety is the key as most dogs will get bored of the same treat day in, day out for all types of activity. A useful tip is to use a few different types of treats, all mixed in together, within a treat pouch. This saves your pockets from smelly crumbs, makes it easy to get the treat out quickly and means that you have a choice of treat to

**ABOVE** A belt-mounted treat pouch is a really useful training accessory. Treats are always readily available to hand, and the durable lining means that crumbly items, like small bits of cheese, can be easily cleaned out at the end of the session.

offer. Normal kibble will also absorb some of the scent and taste from much fancier treats, such as cheese or meat, making the basic biscuit more enticing. There are various treat pouches available. Choose one that suits your style of activity since games that involve you running or jumping around may result in spilled treats or even lost pouches.

**RIGHT** You can enjoy a quick game with a tuggy toy and still retain control of the situation. A retrieve toy is less manageable.

**RIGHT** Only use items of food as treats that are suitable for dogs to eat. Avoid salty crisps and sweets.

Make sure that you only use treats that are suitable for a dog's digestion. There are many options so you should not have to use cookies, chocolates, chips, or sweets made for humans as these could all harm your dog. Dogs with sensitive digestions should be introduced to any new foods slowly and in small amounts to avoid stomach upsets.

**ABOVE** This dog is being asked to Shake A Paw, a game that is described in Chapter 15. Initially you should reward him every time he succeeds. As the game become more familiar to him, the frequency of giving treat rewards can be reduced.

**Reward Schedules** When you first start teaching your dog to do a new activity you must ensure that at first you reward him every time he succeeds. This is important so that he learns to associate the action with the arrival of the reward and so that he stays motivated enough to keep playing, even if the new task is challenging.

## YOUR DOG CAN WIN JACKPOTS!

Occasionally offer your dog a significantly higher reward than normal for an extra good result or positive effort. This will ensure that he remains really enthusiastic about your training. Jackpots should not occur too often

but they are an important part of ultimate training success and enjoyment. You can offer a wonderful type of special treat or many pieces of the regular treat, depending on what your dog will find most appealing. If you are at the end of a longer

**1** This young puppy is in the early stages of training. Here a Sit receives a reward.

training session, your dog may be full and won't appreciate several pieces of treat, so choose jackpots according to the circumstance.

**BELOW** Really special achievements can win a bonus jackpot reward from you.

## REDUCING THE REWARDS

Dropping the reward too early is a common mistake. If you suddenly stop using rewards, your dog may become frustrated and stop performing. Once you have succeeded in getting your dog to perform the action or activity reliably, you can begin to vary your reward schedule. The best way to do this is to offer treats on a more random basis. Initially you should not expect more than three or four repetitions before a reward is offered. However, if you are playing a particularly challenging game, or if there are distractions, you should give rewards more frequently. Praise and petting can always be offered and are a fundamental part of a good dog-owner relationship. Remember that animals work harder and for longer if they know that there is a good chance of a reward eventually.

**2** Next the lure of a treat held in front of his nose is employed to guide the pup into a Stand position.

**3** When the session is over, there is time for some special pats, strokes and words of praise. The young puppy will be keen for more.

# WHAT MOTIVATES YOUR DOG ?

Most owners know roughly what their dog likes but it is always useful to test out your knowledge from time to time since your dog's preferences may change. Being able to understand what really gets your dog motivated is essential and knowing how he grades items is useful when thinking about how to reward simple tasks as opposed to more complex ones. Test your dog with tiny pieces of different treats. Give him a choice of two types (one in each hand) and

LEFT One way of discovering which treat really motivates your dog is to offer him a choice from your left and right hands. Note which one he goes for and let him have it.

preferences. You now know which treat to use for challenging tasks (the favorite) and those which can be used for more simple actions.

**Toy Test** Your dog will be able to tell you which toy is his favorite. When you put all his toys on the floor and let him go and freely play, he is likely to focus on his favorite one. Try this a few times to check for consistency. When you are satisfied which toy is the ultimate playing item, put it away and repeat the process with the remaining toys. You will gradually be able to establish a ranking order for toy preference. Obviously, this is not foolproof since some

BELOW The toy test is another way of establishing a pecking order of favorite playthings. You can then use the most popular as your bumper brain games reward.

note which he chooses to eat first. If he rejects a treat completely then don't choose this as a training reward. Knowing what your dog will choose first lets you rank different rewards according to his

toys are more attractive when being wiggled by a person. You could do the same test using both hands to jiggle two toys at the same time to see which one your dog prefers.

**Owner Focus** Your special attention is probably going to be a highly valuable reward. Earning their owner's praise is a joy to most dogs and it should definitely be a part of all dog training. The reason that we need to use additional rewards, such as treats and toys, is because your dog hears you talking a lot every day. You may be praising your children, or other pets, or chatting on the phone. All these situations expose your dog to your voice when he is doing nothing in particular. This means that the response he then feels when he is praised is slightly lessened by familiarity. However, using a lively and happy tone of voice when you do praise him and clear tones for commands will ensure that your dog understands your desires and that you are pleased.

BELOW Try to keep your voice lively and upbeat when you communicate verbally with your dog. Dull delivery can cause his energy levels to drop.

## WHERE TO BEGIN BRAIN GAMES?

Although you must teach your dog to play in a place where he feels relaxed, you will also have to introduce games in the sorts of environments that you wish your dog to play in. So, for example, if you want your dog to perform a game while out on a walk, then you will probably have to teach the basics at home in a non-distractive environment and then proceed to teach it in new places, such as at the park. If, however, a game is to be played while your dog is home alone, then you should teach him to play within the area in which he will be left. At first you should be present and then gradually leave him to play alone.

LEFT If you want a dog to play a game while left alone at home, teach him the game in the home context.

# WHEN TO BEGIN BRAIN GAMES?

You can begin playing as soon as you are ready. However, it is best to choose a time when you can focus entirely on your dog and when he is feeling fresh and relaxed. Don't start playing with your dog immediately after he has eaten a meal. For starters, he will be less motivated to earn rewards if he is already full. He will also be more likely to want to rest and running or jumping with a full stomach can be dangerous as it could trigger a twist in the intestines which has serious health consequences.

**LEFT** It's not a good idea to start training a brain game immediately after your dog has eaten. He will need some time to digest his food and will not be in the right mood to concentrate.

**BELOW** It's a great trick, but don't expect your dog to be able to balance a biscuit on his nose after just five minutes' training. These game skills need to be built up gradually.

## HAVE REALISTIC AIMS

It is easy to get carried away when you first decide to teach your dog new activities or when you provide him with new toys. Enthusiastic owners often imagine that they are interacting with their own version of Lassie and expect too much too soon, which can be frustrating when the game doesn't go as smoothly as expected. If you are not going to spend lots of time training your dog, then it is unlikely that he will quickly be able to perform all the tricks you desire. Using the brain is very similar to exercising the body; without regular practice they both become slower and less able to work efficiently. If you have not done much with your dog up untill now, don't expect him to suddenly become the canine Einstein overnight. Be patient and consistent and you will get there.

Becoming a good dog handler and trainer takes time and practice. As a dog owner you will develop your

**RIGHT** Not all new toys are instant hits. Don't despair if your puppy seems to lose interest sometimes. It's only natural.

own skills throughout your dog's life so it is worth putting in the effort as early as possible so that you can gain maximum enjoyment out of your time together. You should also have less problem behavior taking up your focus. Even if you have owned dogs before, remember that with each different dog you have to learn about different motivations and instincts. I encourage you to aim high but also to be realistic about your dog's abilities. Some breeds will have more motivation and more physical ability for games than others so you must take these factors into consideration.

Set yourself small achievement goals as this approach will mean you keep having success and so are more likely to continue with your work. Remember that no two dogs are exactly the same and each will enthuse over something different. Try not to compare your dog to your friend's or others in class; they will each have their own special abilities. Some may take longer to learn certain lessons but when they do they may be more reliable than others who picked it up very quickly. Bear in mind that no dog is perfect all of the time.

You should not expect new toys to work miracles or that your dog will spend six hours playing with his new acquisition each day, never again to attempt a naughty

behavior. Habits take time to change and your dog will need to build up his desire to play. Games can extend over long periods, but it is more natural for your dog to play, rest and then play again at intervals during the day. So don't discard the toy too quickly.

This puppy is learning a Sit.

Well done! A good response deserves an immediate reward with a treat.

Now he can be drawn forward into a Stand.

**ABOVE** When you take ownership of a new puppy or adult dog, try to get into the habit of playing simple brain games and teaching basic skills from the outset. It will pay dividends.

## TAKE A BREAK

Puppies and dogs that are new to the training routine should begin learning in very short sessions. Work for up to three minutes then take a break and allow your dog to rest, play a game of his choice or go for a walk. Sessions that are too long will tire him out, make learning less effective and reduce your enjoyment of the session. As your dog matures, or becomes more accustomed to training, you can lengthen the sessions. Of course, once your dog has learned to play his new game, he can be allowed to play it for as long as you deem appropriate. Some games will involve supervised activity, others are designed to keep your dog busy while you are absent from the house or otherwise occupied.

This toy also dispenses treats.

This ball is designed to release small items of food as the dog bats it around the floor with his paws.

**ABOVE** The beauty of activity toys is that they occupy a dog's attention in a rewarding way while it is on its own.

**ABOVE** Don't get too intense when you start to train brain games. Give your dog plenty of breaks and time to rest.

## WHY GOOD GROUND RULES ARE IMPORTANT

In order to play well and safely it is important to have established house rules in place. There are good reasons for this. Firstly, if you spoil your dog he is less likely to work well with you. His motivation for earning rewards or attention will be less and he may be less inclined to interact on your terms. Therefore, it is important to try to establish fundamental ground rules, practice your basic training regularly, hold back on extra treats that haven't been earned by your dog, and try not to give attention just because he demands it. It is also helpful to spend time teaching your dog to take treats and toys from you gently, without grabbing at them. Your dog can have everything he needs — all the attention, fun, petting and treats — but it must be on your terms, not his.

**RIGHT** A clicker is a little hand-operated device that makes a distinctive click noise when a button is depressed. The dog will immediately take notice.

## SHOULD YOU TRY CLICKER TRAINING?

Clicker training is a highly effective method of training which helps owners to "mark" desirable behavior accurately. A clicker is a small plastic device with a metal tongue which makes a "click" when pressed. Since this sound is novel and distinctive, the dog notices it immediately and can easily learn to associate it with a reward. He can also identify what he was doing at the moment when the click occurred and so will repeat this action in order to gain another reward.

**LEFT** You don't want any snatching or nipping when you offer small treats by hand. It's worth taking time to teach your dog how to use his mouth and teeth gently.

Although clicker training does mean you need your clicker to hand, it can make the desired behavior much clearer to the dog. It also encourages you to focus on what your dog is getting right (so you have a trigger that you can "click") rather than just looking for mistakes. This is a much more enjoyable attitude to have when working with him and is much less frustrating for you as a trainer.

**LEFT** This is wrong. The click has come while the dog is lagging behind, not when he is walking to heel.

**ABOVE** Timing is all-important when you start clicker training. You must click at exactly the moment the dog is performing the behavior you want (e.g. walking to heel, above right) and then reward him at once.

There are a couple of ways to use the clicker at this level. Firstly, you can wait for your dog to naturally offer an action or behavior which you then "click." This is often used in behavioral cases when you are trying to correct problem behavior. However, when playing games or training tricks, it can take a very long time for your dog to stumble upon a desirable action. Having said that, dogs can be very creative when they are left to their own devices so you may end up with something much more interesting by using this method. This is especially true if your dog is

accustomed to using his brain to learn new things and has experience of successful trial and error attempts in the past.

## GETTING YOUR TIMING RIGHT

The second way to use your clicker is to initially lure or encourage your dog to move in a certain way or to perform a particular action which you then mark with the click and reward. Once you are getting the action successfully, you slowly fade out your lure and continue to "click" and reward correct efforts. This gets results quickly and is usually the way that we teach tricks and certain doggy sports.

The timing of the click is important as this is your reward cue. The same rules apply as when you're giving praise or offering treats (see page 27).

apply as when you're giving praise or offering treats (see page 27).

**LEFT** Clickers come in many shapes and sizes. There is sure to be one that suits you and your dog.

If you are using a clicker you should make sure that you offer a reward after each click. Initially you will click regularly for small successes. When your dog has improved, you request more and more from him to earn the click. For example, when teaching him to "Shake A Paw" you may click when he raises his paw just a little at first. Then you may hold off clicking until he lifts it slightly higher, then wait for him to actually touch your hand. Eventually he will put his paw in your hand for longer to earn his click and reward. You then have shaped the basics of your trick.

Have fun with your clicker but remember not to click it unless you are trying to reinforce the action your dog is performing. It should also not be played with by children who tend to click at the wrong time or just click to hear the sound themselves. Don't leave it where your dog can find it because a swallowed or chewed clicker is no use to anyone and is potentially very dangerous.

Some sound-sensitive or timid dogs are initially startled by the sound of the clicker. Get round this by either purchasing one of the more modern quiet clickers or try muffling the sound by clicking it inside your sleeve or pocket. It is possible to gradually desensitize a dog to the sound before you begin training and with time and the right rewards, he should begin to associate the sound with things that he likes. Other people successfully train using their own clicking sound which is unlikely to cause any stress.

**BOTH BELOW** A clicker can be used to shape an action bit by bit. This dog is learning to Shake A Paw. Initially just a small paw raise would have been clicked and rewarded. Now the trainer waits for full paw contact before clicking.

The intent look of anticipation shows that the dog is enjoying this game.

# GETTING STARTED WITH A CLICKER

While it is possible to just begin clicking and training straight away, many people like to "tune" their dog to the sound before they start. This is very simple and just involves offering your dog a piece of food and "clicking" just as he takes it. By repeating the "click" and treat combination several times your dog will begin to associate the two, so that when he subsequently hears the "click" he will anticipate the arrival of his treat. While some dogs will make the association after just a few "clicks," others will take a few more sessions. Use this time to get yourself comfortable with using the clicker and to practice your timing.

**ABOVE** You can attune your dog to the sound of the clicker and what it means by "charging" it. Offer your dog a succession of treats and click each time that he takes one. In this way the link between a click and a reward is forged.

# TRAINING WITHOUT A CLICKER

Training without a clicker is perfectly possible too and the game instructions in this book leave it open for you to choose your preferred technique. However, make sure that you focus on giving a specific praise word at exactly the right time to get the best results. There really is a training method to suit everyone.

**BELOW** If you don't plan to use a clicker, it is still possible to train a dog by using other methods. You can achieve the same results with treats and well-timed words of praise.

This dog is being taught to sit up and beg by being lured into position with a treat and then rewarded.

A roll-over can be built up by initially luring a dog over onto its back from a Down position.

# SHAPING BEHAVIORS TO BUILD A GAME

You can't expect your dog to instantly perform a new and complicated brain game. Think about the game and, if possible, break it down into smaller sections which are easier to practice bit by bit. Teach your dog each part separately and then link them together with a chain of commands. "Shaping" is the term that describes the way trainers accept closer and closer approximations of the final actions so that the dog gradually learns to perform the game properly. Since he is rewarded for small improvements along the way, he does not get frustrated and give up if he doesn't succeed quickly.

# BRAIN GAMES INVOLVING TOYS

There is a bewildering choice of toys available which you might buy for your dog to play with. It can be upsetting when your dog chews one up but this should not put you off using toys during

**ABOVE** Some games can be broken down into smaller parts and taught in a modular way by shaping behavior.

play in preference to sticks or stones for the reasons explained below. There are dog toys on the market to suit all budgets, all types of dog and for all types of game.

If you are tired of losing toys while on walks, you need to teach your dog to retrieve reliably. It is useful on such occasions to swap smaller toys for brightly colored ones with rope attachments. These are more easily spotted in the foliage!

**BELOW** Modern dog toys are usually sturdy and brightly colored — ideal for livening up a play session.

# SAFETY CONSIDERATIONS: THE SIZE, SHAPE AND STRUCTURE OF TOYS

Dogs are curious creatures and will investigate new objects, some of which may be dangerous. Indeed, many dogs have to see their vet each year because of injuries sustained while playing. While one of the keys to playing brain games is to use your imagination, you must always consider the safety of the

**RIGHT** Don't buy a small ball for a small dog. Its life could be endangered by accidentally swallowing it.

items you allow your dog to play with. As explained below, the size of toys is important to consider and sharp edges and fragile items are best avoided.

**Size** It is essential that any dog toy is appropriately sized for your dog. Accidental ingestion of balls and other small toys is common and often requires surgery to remove them. If in doubt over a toy, always choose the next size up if one is available. Toys will need regular assessment as your puppy grows because just a few weeks can make the difference between a toy that can or cannot be swallowed. An energetic adolescent is probably more at risk of swallowing a toy during his cavorting play, but you should not take risks with dogs of any age. Be careful if you own dogs of mixed sizes since this will require you to have a mixture of differently sized toys. Where possible, opt for

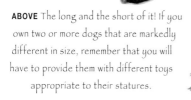

**ABOVE** The long and the short of it! If you own two or more dogs that are markedly different in size, remember that you will have to provide them with different toys appropriate to their statures.

**RIGHT** The cock of the head is so typically canine and it reminds us that dogs are naturally inquisitive. They love to test things with their mouths so take care to choose toys that will be safe.

larger versions and keep smaller balls or activity toys for supervised play only.

**Sticks** are a traditional dog toy but in reality they evoke horror in most veterinarians and dog professionals. The risk of injury from a stick is simply not worth it. When a dog runs after a stick thrown by his owner, he could easily become impaled on a sharp end. Pieces of stick can also break off and lodge in the throat, or splinters can work their way into the body causing severe pain. Since there are many similarly shaped items on the market made from rubber, and an unending number of other fantastic dog toys which cost very little, there is no excuse for using sticks during game play. In general you should avoid all long and sharp items that could cut your dog's mouth, tongue or throat.

**Stones** Another bad habit adopted by some owners who don't have dog toys, or who have forgotten their dog's usual toy, is to throw stones. Typically people choose stones that can be thrown a long way which means that

**ABOVE** This looks like a carefree scene but it is really not advisable to encourage dogs to chase sticks. An over-excited dog might suffer injuries to the mouth or body as a result.
**BELOW** Stones should also be excluded from the playbox. A waywardly thrown stone is a serious health hazard.

they are also small enough to swallow. Dogs that try to catch stones end up with broken or cracked teeth and there is a risk of fatality if the thrown stone accidentally hits the dog's head. Playing with stones can also encourage unwanted focus upon stones which may result in worn teeth. Pebbles can sometimes be ingested in surprisingly large numbers and surgery may be required as a result.

Tough rubber is
a good option.

## OTHER INJURY RISKS

Even commercial toys can be dangerous.
Choose types that can withstand your
dog's strength of bite. If your dog has a
strong desire to chew, then you should
only offer him toys for short play sessions,
taking them away again before he decides
to start chewing them.

**ABOVE** Repeated chewing and biting provide a stern test for dog toys — always look for sturdy, durable examples.

Once a toy has been
damaged, inspect it for
any pieces that might
be swallowed. Rubber
balls that seem solid but
have a hollow center should be avoided.
Without any holes running through the
center to allow free air flow, there is a
very real risk that, if your dog manages
to puncture the toy, the vacuum in the
center may suck in the tongue or other
mouth parts causing severe pain and
possible injury.

Another common
problem occurs when
dogs are given toys
intended for children.
While the toy will have been tested for its
safety with children, this does not mean
that it will hold together in a dog's mouth.
Teddy bears' glass eyes, buttons and
ribbons are among the inappropriate items
that dogs find it interesting to nibble.

If your dog is chewing large chunks off
his toys, you should remove them and try
to find larger, tougher versions. The same

**LEFT** If your dog has a tendency to purloin children's toys for play, remove them. Soft toys are easily pulled apart and small pieces of stuffing or sewn-on decorations can be swallowed. The materials may be toxic or small fragments can get lodged in the dog's airway or intestines.

rule applies to dogs who like to rip the stuffing from their soft toys and chew the squeaker. Since both the squeaker and stuffing can be dangerous if swallowed, it is best to remove and discard the innards yourself. A gutted soft toy can still be perfectly usable once you have done so. Your dog won't care that it no longer resembles the toy in the shop. Alternatively you can buy toys without any stuffing or you can even make your own (see Chapter 4).

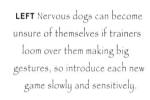

**LEFT** Nervous dogs can become unsure of themselves if trainers loom over them making big gestures, so introduce each new game slowly and sensitively.

# TEACHING BASIC PLAY SKILLS TO TIMID OR NEW DOGS

Some pet dogs lack confidence. Nervousness will inhibit play behavior so it is important that you make sure your dog is as relaxed as possible before you try to teach any game.

If your dog is easily worried, then you should be very careful to introduce new things gradually. How you cope with your dog's sensitivity will depend on what your dog is worried about. You may need to be careful about your movements as some will be anxious if their owners become too exuberant and enthusiastic. Others worry about being in new places or seeing new equipment. The key is to introduce the new thing slowly and steadily while making sure that your dog is enjoying the experience. Relax and give your dog time to learn the rules of the game at a pace that suits him. Undue pressure will make it less likely that your dog will have fun.

**RIGHT** Take things slowly if your dog is a retiring, timid type. Playing brain games should help to boost his confidence but don't overwhelm him with too much too soon.

You may have taken on an adult dog with limited previous experience of toys and fun interactions. These include dogs rescued from puppy farms and some dogs raised for working purposes in kennels. Dogs that have been brought up with other dogs but with limited human contact will lack the skills and knowledge about how to play with a person and so you will have to spend time building up your new dog's trust and carefully introducing play sessions.

If a dog has no play skills, you will need lots of time and patience to show him what to do. Movement is a great way to begin getting a dog interested in a toy.

**LEFT** Some dogs arrive in a household lacking the knowledge of how to interact with people because they have not been properly socialized. First you will have to build up a bond of trust with them.

Wiggling the toy on the floor in small, darting movements is a good place to begin. For small dogs or those who worry about being touched, you can use a cat wand with a furry ending. At first you may just encourage your dog for paying attention to the movement, or for stepping forwards towards it. If he is watching the movement he will probably eventually gain the confidence to move towards it. Short sessions are most productive in such cases. It is slow work but if you can enrich this dog's life with play, it will definitely be worthwhile.

## RESCUED DOGS

If you have taken on a rescue dog, then you should take a little time to allow him to settle in before gently trying out some simple games to see what he likes to do. Don't try to force him to play and if he does play don't try too much at once as you risk overwhelming him. He needs to find his feet and learn to

**BELOW** A cat wand can tempt a dog who does not know how to play with a toy into reacting to the movement of a plaything.

him with more freedom while maintaining your overall control. You must go back and focus on your recall training if this applies to your dog. Try to play and walk in secure areas or places without distraction to make it easier.

**BELOW** If your dog ignores the recall during a game, try using a long training lead.

**ABOVE** Rescue dogs can take time to find their feet in a new home — don't rush things. It probably won't be productive.

trust you. Once you have a feel for his personality and preferences, you can start to really bond over new games together.

# AVOIDING PROBLEMS AND RESOLVING MINOR ISSUES

Playing brain games should be fun and enjoyable for both you and your dog. However, sometimes little problems occur that need to be addressed quickly.

**Running Off** If your dog runs away and won't respond to your call, you will need to keep him on a lead while you play, at least while you teach him that being with you is fun. A long training lead will provide

### HINTS
- Choose a safe area in which to begin playing or to introduce a new toy.
- Allow him to explore and investigate new items or areas before you begin.
- Break the new game into small parts which your dog can easily achieve and reward him well for succeeding.

**ABOVE** Don't get into a pulling match if your dog will not let go of a toy. He needs training, not tug-of-war practice.

**Refusal To Return An Item** If your dog does not want to give up an item, then you need to *stay calm and relaxed*. We tend to get cross and tell our dogs off when they do this but such behavior only results in more anxiety which increases the likelihood that your dog will react badly. Whenever you are teaching a dog to retrieve, be very careful not to immediately grab the item from his mouth.

**LEFT** Your aim must be for the dog to drop the toy into your hand when you ask for it. Be patient and reward good behavior with a treat and lots of praise.

This often makes a dog wary of returning and he will begin to turn his head away from your hand. Praise and pet him first of all, then gently hold his collar with one hand while cupping the item with the other. Wait for him to drop it. Be patient! Your dog's first few experiences of this are important. As he lets go, immediately say "Drop" and praise him profusely. He can then either have a treat or can have the toy thrown again. Using a lead on your dog's collar can prevent him from running away with an item until you teach him that returning is so much more fun.

**ABOVE** There will almost certainly be times when your dog is reluctant to play. Try to motivate him with your voice and body language, but don't force the issue if he is unresponsive.

**Disinterest In The Game** It can sometimes be hard to get a dog in the mood for playing. A major inhibitor is low confidence so make sure your dog feels safe and relaxed. The surrounding

environment should also be free from distraction. This can include other pets and other people. Your own behavior is important so you should act in an excited manner and use a happy voice. Make sure you are trying to play a game that is physically possible for your dog. Break it down into small components and reward him well for showing interest. Try to keep games short at first and make sure he isn't overtired as this will limit his motivation. If your dog has recently eaten or has had several treats, he may also be disinclined to play. Allow him to rest for a while and wait for his appetite to return. If he really does not want to join the game, then perhaps you should think of another game instead. Take time out to rethink what you can do to encourage him to play your first choice of game.

**Too Much Enthusiasm** If you have an energetic dog, allow him to exercise a little before you attempt playing games or training. A lead may give you more control when you do start. In these cases you need to be calm and steady so that you don't encourage extra excitement.

**ABOVE** It's good to keep a training record. It lets you pinpoint areas that need practice and record your successes.

## CHARTING YOUR PROGRESS

Remember that it's not just your dog that needs motivation to engage in games. While it is fantastic to see our dogs improve and learn new things, some of the more difficult tasks take time to achieve. It can sometimes feel as though hardly any progress is being made. Keep a record of how many sessions you have had and describe your training attempts and outcomes as this will give you a more realistic idea about whether or not your dog is getting better, and it may highlight any problem areas that need attention. It is really satisfying to be able to write in that you have finally succeeded!

**RIGHT** Super-energetic dogs may need to let off steam a little before you try to play a brain game.

## USING HAND SIGNALS

Communication is a very complex process and different animals vary immensely between the emphasis they put on visual and vocal signals. As humans, we tend to focus on using words while training our dogs and forget about everything else our bodies are doing. Dogs communicate extensively via body language and movement so it seems very sensible for us to try to consider what our own physical movements may mean and remember that some of our gestures must seem very confusing to our dogs.

While teaching new actions it is useful initially to use a gesture to encourage our dog into position. This lure or movement can later become our reliable hand signal

**ABOVE** : "Please don't hurt me." The smaller dog is using body language to make the classic sign of submission to the Great Dane — rolling onto the back to expose the belly.

or cue for the activity. For example, when we lure our puppies into a "Down," the hand movement that originally encouraged our dog onto the floor becomes a more subtle downward gesture. Since your puppy has experienced the movement alongside the action and has been rewarded for responding to it, he should develop a strong association between the gesture and the action. This allows you to communicate with your dog without the need for words.

This ability is taken advantage of by assistance dog groups who train dogs for people without speech. Dogs are so attuned to their owner's body language that they often respond better to these signals than to words, especially while they are young and just learning to interpret human signals.

**LEFT** The hand signal for Down.

**RIGHT** The Down is usually taught by using a treat to lure a dog into the desired position. As the lesson is learnt, the treat is eliminated. The hand signal becomes the visual cue.

# INTRODUCING VERBAL CUES

While our body language is very important to dogs, we can't really escape the need to add verbal signals too. Dogs can learn to respond to their owner's vocal signals impressively well. There are records of dogs who can correctly respond to over 200 different word cues given by their owner. While this may seem like an unachievable target, your dog will be able to learn a range of verbal cues if you practice enough.

The first mistake when using word cues is to try to shout it repeatedly at the dog. Stop and remember that unless you have taught

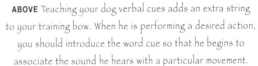

**ABOVE** Teaching your dog verbal cues adds an extra string to your training bow. When he is performing a desired action, you should introduce the word cue so that he begins to associate the sound he hears with a particular movement.

your dog properly, he won't have any idea about what this sound you are making actually means. Be patient. The word cue should not be introduced until your dog is actually performing the action you want to associate with it. Your dog effectively has to learn a new language when he interacts with you. It is very easy for him to make mistakes if you don't make the message absolutely crystal clear.

**LEFT** The ability of dogs to interpret human body language is made clear when you watch an assistance or therapy dog in action. Some dogs are so sensitive to their owners' needs that they function like an extra pair of eyes, ears and hands.

A common scenario is to shout "Sit!" at a puppy that is jumping up at you. From this experience your puppy learns that jumping and the sound "Sit" always occur together. This does not teach him to "Sit." In fact, it makes it more likely that he will continue to jump or at least fail to respond to your "Sit" command.

The right way is to teach him to sit by luring and rewarding the action first. When he is sitting you should introduce the

**1** This is how to teach a puppy what "Sit" should mean to him.

**2** Firstly you get his attention with a treat in your hand. Then you slowly move it back up and over his head.

**LEFT** Shouting at a puppy to "Sit" when he is jumping up at you only confuses the issue. The command "Sit" should be linked to a situation when the pup has his haunches squarely on the ground. You don't want him to think that "Sit" = Jump.

**3** When he drops into a sit position, say "Sit" and immediately reward. Through repetition, the verbal cue becomes the trigger for the action.

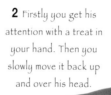

word "Sit." Link the action and the sound together enough times and he will begin to understand. Gradually you should begin to give your word cue just before your puppy responds to your hand signal or lure. He will learn that when he hears the sound "Sit" he should do this sitting action as he will then be rewarded. If you teach in this order, when your puppy does jump up you can calmly ask him to "Sit" and he will remember what he is meant to do and respond correctly.

Also remember: don't repeat your command word over and over again if it does not produce the required response the first time round. Give the dog time to think and react, especially when you first begin training. Repeating it several times in a row tends to fail as the dog begins to respond to this chain of words rather than the single intended word. So instead of a simple "Sit" getting the desired response, you then have to say "Sit-sit-sit-sit."

It also runs the risk of your dog becoming completely desensitized to that word or linking it with something else that he is doing or seeing. If you think any of these problems are occurring, then take a step back and try to consider why he is not responding. If your dog is distracted, then gain his attention before you give your command clearly. Watch your body language and pay attention to the tone of your voice, since if you're frustrated your dog might read these signals and also become stressed.

## MINIMIZING CUES

When you first teach a command you are likely to use large gestures and exaggerated lures. As your dog begins to understand what the game is about, you can begin to minimize the signals that you give. All gestures can be gradually minimized. Practice the task that you want your dog to perform and after a couple of repetitions your dog will begin to anticipate what you are asking for just as you begin to give your signal. Each time use a slightly shortened version of the hand signal and make sure that you reward your dog immediately for responding. Challenge yourself and your dog to work with minimal cues since this is really impressive to observers.

**RIGHT** Most dogs pick up lessons remarkably quickly. Before long your puppy will be happy to sit when you give even quite small gestures as cues.

**ABOVE** The best-laid plans... There will be times when you are teaching a brain game when things just do not go as you want them to.

## COPING WHEN TRAINING DOESN'T GO AS PLANNED

It can be really frustrating when you can't get what you want from a training session. When people get frustrated they are more likely to make mistakes, use inconsistent methods, push the dog too hard and resort to punishment.

If your dog is not picking up the lesson you are trying to teach him, then stop, take a step back and really think about what you are doing. He isn't picking it up for a reason and usually that reason is that the handler is not making the message clear. If your dog has been trying unsuccessfully for a while, you should take a break and allow him to relax. Check that your rewards are highly motivating and go through all the possible reasons for his lack of interest.

## AVOID PUNISHMENT DURING GAMES

Brain games are meant to be fun and should not require punishment. When your dog makes a mistake, stop the game and try again. If he repeatedly makes a mistake, then he has misunderstood the task you are setting him. Retrace your steps and make sure he is performing the early stages successfully. If your dog becomes

Now the cane is set lower, hopping over it is a piece of cake.

**ABOVE** It helps when you are having problems to go back a stage or two in the game to re-establish the basics.

over-excited or behaves in an unacceptable way, then stop the game. Allow him to calm down while you consider what went wrong. Getting angry and punishing him is likely to make him even more frantic or scared and could exacerbate any problem behavior.

Your dog may become frustrated if he doesn't get a reward when he expects it. This may be because the rules of the game have suddenly changed or because he is confused. Remember to help him to achieve for the first few times and then gradually reduce your input while letting him think the game through for himself. If your dog is confused, you will probably see him trying lots of different actions that have previously earned him rewards. Try not to tell him off for these mistakes, just make sure you don't reward him for performing actions you haven't asked for. Wait for a moment to give him a chance to think it through and if necessary then go back a stage and help him to perform the correct task.

# BEING PREPARED TO PLAY

Each brain game description in this book is accompanied by a list of the items or props that you will require. It pays to be prepared before starting each game, especially those you have made up yourself. Decide on

what you need, if you need helpers, what your command word will be and where you should begin training.

**Equipment Check** You are responsible for your dog's safety at all times so choose any equipment you use carefully. Basic training tools such as your dog's collar or harness should be fitted correctly and free from

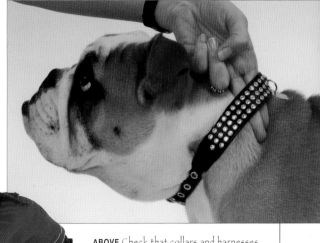

**ABOVE** Check that collars and harnesses are in good condition and fit properly.

damage. Official canine sports will have their own recommended equipment so you should do your research and talk to other team members to find out what you need to join in.

**LEFT** If you need any special props to play the games in this book, the boxed tables will tell you.

# LET THE

# PART TWO

# BRAIN GAMES BEGIN

# IT'S PUPPY-PLAY

A puppy will normally have lots of energy and enthusiasm for games. However, without guidance, the games your puppy chooses to play may not be appropriate since they like to use their mouths and to jump and chase. This is not suitable if the puppy is biting your hands or chasing your toes. By teaching your puppy to play properly, it will start to direct its biting onto its toys. Don't just expect your puppy to play properly with the toys you buy; spend time gently encouraging him and praising him for getting it right.

| | SOLO GAME<br>Dog alone |
|---|---|
| **LOCATION** | Anywhere where your puppy may be tempted to chew on something else. |
| **LEVEL OF DIFFICULTY** | ☆ Easy brain exercise |
| **PROPS** | A variety of items to chew on. |

# PUPPY CHEW CHEW

All puppies need to chew while they are growing up. Some breeds are naturally more mouthy than others and most have the potential to create a lot of damage to your home or possessions. Chewing is a natural and normal activity so don't expect your puppy never to chew anything; instead teach him to focus on his own playthings.

### SUITABLE CHEW TOYS
Provide your puppy with a selection of toys of different shapes, sizes and textures. He is likely to have specific preferences but favorite items can change depending on his mood, whether he is teething or if he's hungry. You will have to spend time encouraging any dog to play with a new item and young puppies have to learn how to use some of the activity toys properly.

### CHEWIES
There are a range of chews available on the market which will occupy your puppy. Supervision is essential while your puppy is playing with these as some pups will try to swallow them whole in their excitement.

### RAWHIDE CHEW ITEMS
Rawhide chews made from cow skin come in all sorts of shapes and sizes. For ultimate safety choose rawhides made in a country with trusted safety standards and remove any small pieces to prevent choking. Vary the shapes of the rawhide chews you buy for added interest.

### PUPPY ACTIVITY TOYS

Many of these toys are made from durable rubber soft enough for your puppy's mouth. Be careful to exchange these for adult versions once your puppy grows up. These toys usually work by having a hollow center which you fill with your pup's dinner or some treats which he then has to spend time getting out to enjoy.

### ENCOURAGING ACTIVITY PLAY

Make this easy at first or he may give up. Praise and encourage him to play with the toy. You might need to hold it at first while he starts to lick the food from the center. Eventually he will be happy to take the toy and play by himself. Remember to keep encouraging him and occasionally pop another enticing treat inside. Practice your retrieve game with one of these and take the opportunity to add more food when your pup brings the toy to you. If you get it right, he should be happy to spend prolonged periods playing with his toys.

### NYLABONE PUPPY CHEWS

Specially designed for young puppies without adult teeth and strength, the nylabone puppy products provide safe options for your puppy's chewing urges. They are available in edible and non-edible options to suit your dog. Graduate to adult nylabone products when your puppy matures.

# PUPPY RETRIEVE

It may seem completely natural to see a dog chasing a toy and bringing it back to his owner. However many dogs never learn to do this and their owners end up retrieving all the toys they throw. Teach your puppy to perform a simple retrieve and there are many more advanced games that you can move on to later.

| | INTERACTIVE GAME |
|---|---|
| | Dog and Owner |
| **LOCATION** | In a low-distraction area to start with. |
| **LEVEL OF DIFFICULTY** | ☆ ☆ Moderate brain tester |
| **PROPS** | A favorite toy, treats or another toy to swap it with. |

**THE BASIC RETRIEVE GAME**

**1** Don't make the mistake of throwing the toy a long way when your puppy is tiny. You can begin by rolling a ball or tossing a toy just a very short distance away.

**2** As your puppy grabs the toy you should call encouragement, "Good dog!," and behave excitedly which should encourage him to run back to you holding the toy.

**BUILDING UP THE SKILL**

Repeat the game shown on the right (**1-4**) just a few times during each session or your puppy may become bored or tired. Take a break and play again later. Practice with different toys and in different places so that your puppy learns the game properly.

You may be concerned about more formal presentation of items later on but during the early stages you should focus on making sure your dog loves bringing things back to you rather than exactly how he drops them. This can be learned later if you want to take up more official working or obedience dog training.

If you find that your puppy has a tendency to run away with the toy, you can either tie a light line to the toy or attach a puppy house-line to your pup's collar. These can be used to prevent your pup from

running away but don't ever drag him towards you. This technique is also useful for older dogs that have already learned unwanted habits.

Over time, as your puppy improves, you can throw the toy farther and farther. If you are a particularly bad thrower or suffer from shoulder problems, you may find it easier to use a ball on a rope or even a purpose-made ball launcher to help you achieve greater distances.

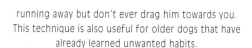

**TIP** Don't get caught in a tuggy game with your puppy unless you want that to happen. Keep your hand still and close to your body and you'll find that he eventually gives up since tuggy is not very exciting if you're not playing too.

**3** Try to present your reward only once he has returned, as many puppies will drop the toy as soon as they spot the treat that you are offering. Avoid grabbing the toy from your puppy's mouth. Take a moment to praise him for returning to you, gently cup the toy in one hand while offering a treat with the other hand. The moment your pup lets go of the toy you can say "Drop" or another chosen command word and offer the treat.

**4** Some dogs prefer to swap for another toy. If your puppy is reluctant to let go, stay relaxed. If you get impatient and tense, he will too which will make it less likely that he will let go.

Just wait and keep your voice soft and your face relaxed. Eventually he will let go and then you can reward him so that he will be keen to let go even more quickly next time.

# GO TO BED

Most owners want to be able to ask their dogs to go and lie down quietly. This makes entertaining your guests or working from home more relaxing as you can easily send your dog away when you don't want him demanding attention or jumping on you.

| | INTERACTIVE GAME |
|---|---|
| | **Dog and Owner** |
| **LOCATION** | Start near your puppy's bed and then in other places where you would like him to settle. |
| **LEVEL OF DIFFICULTY** | ☆ ☆ **Moderate brain tester** A "Down" command will be useful. |
| **PROPS** | Puppy bed, treats and chewies. |

Unfortunately, sending a dog to his bed is often done in the form of a telling off rather than a fun game. If you spend a little time teaching your dog to rush to his bed and lie down to earn a reward, you will find him more reliable, easier to live with and you can also use this technique for other training tasks.

You can choose to teach your puppy to go and lie on his bed. This must be a place that he feels happy about going to, so reward him well for using it when told to. Start with sessions during which your puppy is unlikely to be distracted. You'll be more successful if you practice during quieter times rather than only when he's wound up or excited.

**LURE AND REWARD**

**1** Begin with your puppy standing beside you while you crouch down a foot or so from his bed. Toss a nice treat into the bed to act as a lure to start the training.

**2** Allow your puppy to go forwards after the treat. When he climbs into his bed praise him and throw in another treat. To practice again either wait until he leaves his bed or call him out and repeat the routine.

**3** At this stage it doesn't matter if your puppy is just standing on his bed or lying down when you reward him. Your first aim is to teach him that going to that place is fun.

### INTRODUCE A "DOWN"

The next step is to get your puppy to lie down on his bed before you offer the reward.

Puppies are remarkably quick to learn what you want them to do, especially when there is a reward.

Some puppies will require you to lure them into position at first depending on the amount of practice you have done on the "Down" command prior to training this. As soon as he lies down, give him his treat.

Practice sending him to his bed again to help him learn that he now has to also lie down to earn that treat. Once your puppy understands, he'll be more likely to get into position faster.

## INTRODUCING YOUR VERBAL COMMAND

Now he is doing the action you want, you can introduce your verbal command. Next time he gets onto the bed say "Go to bed," then praise him. You can then toss another treat to him for remaining there and say your "Go to bed" phrase again. You will need to repeat this stage several times to help him make the association. Try to practice a few times a day for a couple of minutes each time.

Now practice without tossing the first treat. Your puppy will be familiar with the throwing gesture now and this can be shaped into your signal for "Go to bed." As he approaches the bed say "Go to bed" and then, once he has hopped in, praise him and toss the treat into the bed as a pleasant reward.

> **TIP** Your puppy will build lots of positive associations with being in his bed area so eventually you will not have to offer treats. However, this is the ideal place to offer chews and activity toys no matter how old your dog becomes.

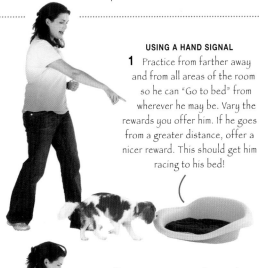

### USING A HAND SIGNAL

**1** Practice from farther away and from all areas of the room so he can "Go to bed" from wherever he may be. Vary the rewards you offer him. If he goes from a greater distance, offer a nicer reward. This should get him racing to his bed!

**2** Begin to increase the time he has to spend in his bed. To encourage him to remain there for longer, offer him additional chews or a puppy activity toy in his bed. Ideally you will teach him to remain in his bed until you tell release him with your "Off you go" command or call him out.

# TAKE IT AND LEAVE IT

All dogs should be able to respond to a command which tells them that they should stop whatever they are doing. We call this "Leave it" which is a game of urge control. It is best to reinforce this command during short training sessions as you'll then have more chance of success in situations where it's vital that your puppy obeys. It will also make it easier to play some of the more advanced brain games in this book.

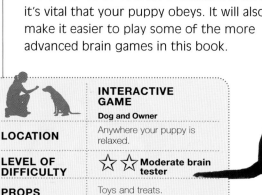

| | **INTERACTIVE GAME** | |
|---|---|---|
| | Dog and Owner | |
| **LOCATION** | Anywhere your puppy is relaxed. | |
| **LEVEL OF DIFFICULTY** | ☆ ☆ | Moderate brain tester |
| **PROPS** | Toys and treats. | |

**TEACHING THE "LEAVE IT" PART OF THE GAME**

**1** Begin by holding a toy that your puppy likes but don't start with his ultimate favorite plaything. Wiggle the toy around to excite his interest.

By teaching your puppy the concept of "Leave it" in the following positive way, he will remain happy when he hears the command rather than feeling worried when you have to shout it for the first time during an emergency. This will make his response more reliable. Practice for short sessions each day until he is excellent.

The "Take It" part involves nice manners. Your puppy will learn to wait until instructed before taking something from your hand. This can be very useful when there are children in the house or when a dog is a little too enthusiastic

about grabbing toys or treats. This follows on very naturally from the "Leave it" part of the game.

**1** Most dogs pick up the "Leave it" lesson up very quickly. Practice with food and chewies too.

**TIP** This is one lesson where you can introduce the verbal cue early. Puppies learn this so quickly that it seems to make little difference if you wait until he has backed away before saying the "Leave it" cue. Just make sure you only reward him for the right response.

**3** Wait for him to let go or to move back very slightly and then immediately reward him with a treat or toy from your other hand while saying "Take it."

**2** If he tries to take it from you, stop moving the toy and tell him to "Leave it."

**4** Make sure he is not pawing at you before you offer the reward. As you practice, he should begin to move away farther or cease pawing you more promptly when you give your "Leave it" command.

**2** Your puppy should eventually begin to generalize the "Leave it" term as being a signal to stop what he's doing and back off since he knows that doing so will bring a reward.

**3** Once he has stopped mouthing the hand as you have instructed him to, you can deliver the treat with the other hand.

# GAMES AT HOME

One of the main places where your dog needs stimulation is within the home environment. These games will help to keep your dog occupied when he is left alone or when you have visitors, while some can even be useful if you want your dog to help around the house!

## ACTIVITY TOYS AND BOREDOM BUSTERS

There are numerous toys on the market that are designed to occupy your dog for long periods while he attempts to get at the food you have stuffed inside.

| | SOLO GAME<br>Dog alone |
|---|---|
| **LOCATION** | Anywhere although less appropriate on light carpets because of mess and possible saliva stains. |
| **LEVEL OF DIFFICULTY** | ☆ ☆ **Moderate brain tester** |
| **PROPS** | A range of toys suitable for your dog's size and jaw strength. Food to stuff inside. |

There are options out there to suit any dog's size or preference so all dogs can learn to use these given enough time. The purpose of these toys is to encourage your dog to use up time in order to access his food while taking advantage of his natural foraging instincts. It's far too common for a dog only to have to walk as far as his food bowl or look at you in a certain way to receive a free flow of food. This is far from natural and leaves your dog with a lot of spare time to get into mischief. In a natural situation your dog would have to find prey, hunt it down and then spend quite a bit of time chewing and working on ingesting the food. Pet dogs have a much less gruesome task, but their basic instincts are still there and by making the feeding process as interesting as possible, they should feel more satisfaction. It also means that they use up extra energy while making a small amount of food last longer. This is great for dogs that appear to be constantly hungry or that need to lose weight. Cutting back on the amount you feed your dog won't be so obvious if you feed its ration via an activity toy rather than the bowl.

**LOAD THE FOOD**

Begin by stuffing the toy with a foodstuff that you know he likes (and you know won't upset his digestion). If you are using dry kibble make it less likely to fall out all at once by forcing in some larger pieces of dog biscuit to block the exit. Inserting softer foods alongside the kibble will help to bind the dry food together which will also make it last longer. Small amounts of soft cheese or pâté can be smeared around the aperture to encourage your dog to forage.

### MAINTAIN VARIETY

Make these toys interesting by varying the fillings, swapping them with different styles and only offering them at certain times, rather than having them available all day every day. Most are very easy to clean once your dog has finished playing. Remember to refill it again next time though as an empty toy will not keep him occupied to anything like the same extent.

**TIP** If your dog is still getting a bowl full of food at its mealtimes, it may be less inclined to bother working for extras from food toys. This depends on how motivated your dog is to get at food. By feeding the main meals from these toys or by making the food inside the toys much higher value than the normal meals, your dog's motivation to play will soar.

### A GOOD USE FOR THOSE FOOD SCRAPS

Extra interest can be gained by placing any food scraps from the kitchen intended for your dog inside the toy too.

### GET YOUR DOG INTERESTED IN THE TOY

Hold the toy while your dog sniffs and licks it and offer praise when your dog shows interest. Don't expect simply to present the new toy to your dog and for him to know exactly what to do straight away. Most dogs need to be shown and encouraged to use the toy at first. While he is licking it, introduce the name for the toy, for example "Kong!" This is useful for your word games later on.

Your dog will soon build an association between the toy and the enjoyment he's had with it and this will build up his endurance for playing with it until it's emptied.

# ACTIVITY TOYS

No matter what your dog's style of play or preference for shape is, there will be an activity toy to suit. Some toys can be rolled or thrown like balls, while others have irregular shapes that make them move unpredictably. Those with grooved surfaces can even rub on the surfaces of your dog's teeth, helping to keep them clean while he plays. Several types of doggy board game have been developed. These can be simple or highly complex depending upon how much time you want to spend training and how keen your dog is to learn. Some require supervision, so choose carefully and select safe toys that your dog can play with alone if that's your main requirement.

Dogs need to work at it to get their treats.

### KONG

This popular rubber toy is available in two different strengths and in various sizes to suit most dogs. For a hard chewer choose the tougher black version and select a larger size. These can be heated in the microwave or frozen to create tempting distractions.

### STUFFABALL

This ridged rubber toy can be used as a ball or a food dispenser. The shape provides a variation to the Kong toys. The red version will suit normal dogs though the tougher black rubber one should be bought for stronger jawed dogs.

### CANINE GENIUS

This new version of the rubber activity toy provides a novel shape and allows you to link several toys together which makes it more difficult for your dog to work the treats out. This provides a better challenge for the dogs who are professionals at emptying their Kong toy.

### TREAT BALL

This hard plastic ball can be filled with your dog's dry food. He will have to move about the room, rolling the toy with his nose or paw to dispense the treats.

### DOGGY PYRAMID

The hole at the top of this plastic pyramid-shaped toy allows treats to fall out when it is pushed over. The weighted base allows the toy to re-right itself after your dog knocks it over, which means that he has to push it again to get more food to tip out.

### BUSTER BONE

This plastic bone-shaped treat toy has a hole at one end where the treats can drop out. Your dog's instincts will encourage him to hold the bone and sniff at the opening. However, he actually needs to tip the toy upside down for the food to come out so it provides more interest and occupies him for longer.

### BUSTER CUBE

This is a cubic version of the Treat Ball. Internal cavities slow down the release of the treats while your dog rolls it around on the floor. Different sizes are available to suit different dogs. It is also possible to alter the difficulty to challenge more advanced dogs. Small versions may become stuck in large dog's jaws so opt for the larger version if in doubt.

### BOARD GAMES

More complex purpose-made games have been available for lucky dogs. These vary from boards that your dog has to paw at to slide open compartments, or to spin a disc, to those where he has to learn to remove blocks to open the compartments. There's bound to be a version that your dog enjoys.

The dog must spin the disc to get to the hidden treats.

# HOMEMADE BOREDOM BUSTERS

If you are creative, it is possible to make your own versions of some of the activity toys, although the commercially available ones are durable and have been tested for safety and toxicity. They tend to be good value for your money.

## PLASTIC BOTTLES

If your dog is not particularly destructive, then you may have success with empty plastic bottles or milk cartons containing pieces of dry food which can then be left on the floor for your dog to roll around and jump on. The top should be removed so your dog cannot swallow it and to allow the food to fall out gradually. If it is chewed and cracked, be careful that there are no sharp edges that could cut your dog's mouth and that he is not chewing off and swallowing small pieces. The bottle should be replaced regularly.

## RAGGY TREAT TOY

Soft raggy toys are often loved by small dogs who like to chew and shake them. These can be easily made up at home and can be made really interesting by including treats within the fabric. Plait up strips of an old sheet or tea-towel with treats bound up inside. Your dog can then chew and rag this up. Take care that your dog cannot swallow bits of the fabric.

**1** This toy is a great option for owners who regularly have to replace ragger toys that their dog chews up during his teething stages. Begin by cutting a spare tea towel into long strips.

**2** Take three long strips of fabric and tie them together at one end with a secure knot.

**3** Now start to plait the strips together by passing them alternately over and under one another. Treats can be included too.

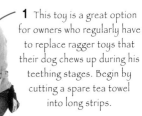

### MAKING A HANGING TREAT DISPENSER

Plastic bottles can also be hung up so that your dog has to pull and bat them about to get the food out. Carefully make a hole in the bottom end and thread through a cord (or an elasticized strap) that you will use to attach the bottle to a door handle or even for hanging the toy in the garden. Tie a knot in the end of the cord so it holds the bottle securely. It should hang with the hole pointing downwards. Treats can either be fed in through the natural bottle top or you can cut a letterbox hole at the top end of the bottle.

### TIME FOR PLAY

The selection of treats used in this hanging toy needs some thought or the game will be over within a moment. Choose longer bone-shaped biscuits and larger kibble that don't fall out on the first shake of the bottle. If you have a small dog or want to use smaller treats, you can also insert scrunched up paper into the bottle to slow down the dispensing of the treats.

### NOW FOR SOME FUN

You can begin the game by wiggling the toy on the floor or encouraging your dog to take it in his mouth. Praise him for starting to play.

This toy also works to tempt dogs to show an interest in playing with normal ragger toys if you are trying to teach some simple play skills. Choose a name for this toy such as "Raggy" for using later in your word games.

**4** When you get to the other end, again secure the loose ends with a secure knot.

**5** The finished toy with a number of tempting treats concealed within the plaited strands.

# FIND IT

A Find It game will encourage your dog to use his nose to provide him with stimulation and distraction. While gundogs will be especially good at this game, it is one that all breeds will be able to learn and enjoy to some level.

**1** One person should gently hold your dog by his collar or lead while you show him a favorite treat (or toy if preferred). Remain in sight while you place the treat under something easily moved such as a cushion.

| | INTERACTIVE GAME |
|---|---|
| | **Dog and Owner** |
| **LOCATION** | Any location with safe places to hide items. |
| **LEVEL OF DIFFICULTY** | ☆ ☆ ☆ |
| | **Good brain workout** |
| **PROPS** | Some dry treats, a toy, a helper may be useful during the early stages. |

**TIP** Avoid really smelly treats as they will leave strong scents behind where they've been hidden. This could encourage your dog to go through your possessions unbidden at a later time which may not be safe.

# THE LEG WEAVE

Teaching your dog to weave in and out of your legs is a fun game that can get you both into a bit of a tangle at first. The aim of this game is for your dog to weave in a figure eight around your legs. The hand movements can be tricky to get right at first but soon your dog will be weaving through your legs with ease.

**1** Stand up with your legs apart. Hold a treat in each hand. Lure your dog through your legs from front to back using the treat in your right hand. As your dog follows your hand through your legs, you should lure him around the outside of your right leg to the front. At this point you can offer the treat. Continue the weave by bringing your left hand behind your left leg and lure your dog back through your legs and round the outside towards the front again so completing the figure eight. Offer your treat as he completes the move.

| | INTERACTIVE GAME |
|---|---|
| | **Dog and Owner** |
| **LOCATION** | Anywhere you can stand while your dog moves around you. |
| **LEVEL OF DIFFICULTY** | ☆ **Easy brain exercise** |
| **PROPS** | Treats (and a stick or another person for Extended Leg Weave). |

**BUILD THE SKILL**
Keep practicing by tucking treats behind chairs or in other safe locations within the room. Don't move to harder places until your dog can easily "Find it" at this level.

**2** Your helper should then release your dog to run forwards to get the treat. If you don't have a helper, then try putting your dog behind a dog gate or attach his lead to something solid to keep him in place but still in view.

**3** He'll probably use his nose or paw to move the item hiding the treat. Say "Find it" as he finds the treat. For more advanced dogs that know a reliable "Stay," use the command to keep them in place if you cannot call on the assistance of a helper.

**2** Your command word may be "Through" or "Weave" and should be introduced once your dog is moving comfortably through your legs. Remember to praise your dog to keep the game fun.

With practice you will be able to point and ask your dog to "Weave" without holding food in your hands. Try not to ask for too many weaves without rewarding your dog at first or he may become tired of the game.

**THE EXTENDED LEG WEAVE**
Once you have taught a basic leg weave you can extend this to include a stick or even another person. This is harder as you do not have both hands free to signal your dog to weave (unless you have a free-standing item to weave around). If you have a friend available to help, then ask them to stand in a line next to you with their legs apart. This game requires team work and good timing by both trainers.

The weave can be as long as you want it to be so no one in the family needs to be left out!

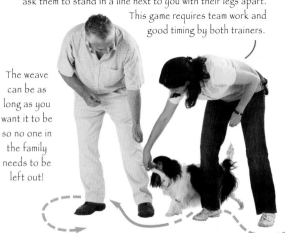

# JUMP OVER

You can start this game once your dog is physically mature and if he is fit enough for jumping. This game can be transferred outside to become part of your own obstacle course (see Chapter 6) or you might then become interested in joining an agility group (see Chapter 16).

| | **INTERACTIVE GAME**<br>Dog and Owner |
|---|---|
| **LOCATION** | In a room with some open floor space or an open doorway. |
| **LEVEL OF DIFFICULTY** | ☆ **Easy brain exercise** |
| **PROPS** | Treats, something to jump such as a broom handle, plastic pole, garden cane or walking stick. Blocks or cones to rest the pole on at suitable heights. |

**JUMP OVER**

**1** Start by placing your pole on the floor. You should allow your dog some space to approach the pole and make sure that the floor surface is suitable for jumping and landing on.

**LIMBO DANCING**

**1** This time begin with the pole raised high in your hand. Encourage your dog to walk underneath it by either luring with a treat or by rolling a toy under the bar. Reward him with a treat or allow him to get the toy you rolled if he prefers. Repeat and introduce your command word "Under."

**2** Very gradually you should lower the pole until it is resting on the supports. Practice encouraging your dog underneath in the same way. Repeat until your dog is comfortable at each level.

# LIMBO DANCING

While you have your pole for jumping to hand, you can also teach your dog another game using the same equipment. It is a good idea to teach one command at a time so that he has a thorough understanding of each one before you risk confusing him with a different action.

☆ ☆ **Moderate brain tester**

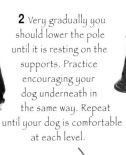

**3** As your dog grows in confidence, you can raise the pole very gradually. How high you raise the bar will depend upon the size and fitness of your dog. Be sensible over how high you ask him to jump.

**2** Lure your dog over the pole to make sure that he is comfortable around this new piece of equipment. Once he is, you can start to slowly raise it off the floor. Hold the pole just an inch or so off the floor at first. Lure your dog over the pole and praise him for getting it right. Repeat the "Jump" at this height until your dog seems very comfortable. As he goes over give your command word "Jump" or "Over." Reward your dog for successfully crossing the jump each time.

**TIP** It may be easier to prop your pole on some books or chairs to free up your hands while you train. For safety purposes you should ensure that the pole can easily be knocked off if your dog bumps into it accidentally.

**3** Start to say your command word just as he dips his head down. As your dog improves, he will become better at getting lower and lower to crawl underneath the pole without knocking it off its supports.

**TIP** If you ask your dog to go "Under" and he goes over, or vice versa, you should not reward him. Try again, making it a little easier to get it right and reward him well when he succeeds.

**2** Once your dog is confidently going under the pole, you can tie on another strip. Keep adding them until your dog can happily push or crawl through the strips.

**LIMBO FOR THE MORE ADVENTUROUS DOG**

**1** If you want to make this game a little more adventurous, tie ribbons or strips of material to the pole. It takes confidence for a dog to push through these. Begin with just a few widely spaced strips. Start with the pole high enough for your dog to be able to walk beneath it.

1 First teach your dog to go and "Sit" in your chosen place.

2 This can be made easier if you choose to focus your dog on a mat or rug as this will act as a visual reminder. Your command can be something like "On your mat."

# DOORBELL DASH

Most dogs become excited when they hear the doorbell since they associate the sound with the arrival of visitors. They often dash around barking, getting under your feet and then leap up at the guests as they enter your home.

| | **INTERACTIVE GAME**<br>Dog and Owner |
|---|---|
| **LOCATION** | Inside your home. |
| **LEVEL OF DIFFICULTY** | ☆ ☆ ☆ ☆<br>**Advanced brain game**<br>A reliable "Sit" will be useful. |
| **PROPS** | Doorbell (or knocker), a helper, treats, a pre-stuffed activity toy. |

This game teaches dogs to respond in a different, more manageable way when they hear the doorbell. They learn to go to a specific place when they hear the doorbell so they can earn their reward.

While this can help with unruly dogs, if your dog is aggressive towards people then you must make sure that he cannot get to your guests as they enter your home.

Begin by deciding where you would like your dog to go when the doorbell rings:

**FRIENDLY DOG**

If your dog is very friendly and just needs to learn some manners, you might be happy for him to meet your guests directly at the door. Often the chosen spot is at the foot of the staircase or in an area where he is out of the way as the door opens and guests come in.

**UNFRIENDLY DOG**

If your dog is not always friendly or is at risk of escaping from the house when the door opens, you may choose to teach him to rush to another room instead. This will mean that you no longer have to drag him there when the bell rings.

**3** Remember to reward him for going to the right place. Once he can do this easily you can introduce the doorbell sound cue.

**4** When you first ring the bell your dog is likely to rush off to the door. Stay calm and wait for him to focus on you. Encourage him back onto his mat. When he responds correctly make sure you reward him well.

If you practice the above steps (**1-4**) enough, he will link the sound of the doorbell with the new action that he has learned knowing that it will bring him rewards. He should respond correctly when he hears the doorbell in the future.

The next step is to begin to open the door without anyone on the other side. Teach him to remain in place as you open the door an inch at a time. If he remains in place, reward him. Gradually increase the distance you open the door before rewarding him.

If you are worried about him rushing forwards and possibly out of the door, you can use a temporary training line to prevent this from being possible. When he goes into position, loop the end of the line to the stair rail or even just hold on to the end.

**INTRODUCE ANOTHER PERSON**

Finally practice with another person behind the door. First of all they should stay quiet and walk in calmly, ignoring your dog. You can give him his reward as they pass by. Practice often with familiar friends and family who will understand what you are trying to teach. Avoid trying to include a busy delivery man as he probably won't have time to help you train.

**TIP** A final touch to the "Doorbell Dash" is to keep a pre-stuffed activity toy or tempting chewy near the front door. When your dog behaves nicely and allows visitors in while remaining calm, he can be given the toy. This will continue to distract him while you entertain your guests and ensure that he just loves having people come around.

# WHERE ARE MY KEYS?

Every one of us has had to search around for our keys at some point and some of us have realized with horror that we have dropped our keys while out walking. Improve the chances of finding your keys quickly by teaching your dog to help you search for them. Some dogs will have better instincts for this game than others but have a go and see how far you progress with your dog.

| | INTERACTIVE GAME |
|---|---|
| | **Dog and Owner** |
| **LOCATION** | In your home first and then on walks for advanced canines. |
| **LEVEL OF DIFFICULTY** | ☆ ☆ ☆ |
| | **Good brain workout** |
| | Teach "Find it" and "Retrieve" first. |
| **PROPS** | Keys, key-ring, soft toy or handkerchief. |

**PLEASE ADD HEADING**

First of all you must make sure that your dog can easily find and pick up your keys. This is easier if you attach a soft item to your key-chain. This may be a soft toy, handkerchief or even just a large leather key-fob. These are easier for your dog to detect and pick up than a bunch of metal keys alone.

**THE INITIAL RETRIEVE**

**1** Play a "Retrieve" game with the keys to begin with. Make them exciting by jiggling them about on the floor and giving lots of praise when your dog shows an interest in picking them up. When he does, say the cue "Keys!" and then tell him he is a good boy when he fetches them.

### NOW ADD THE "FIND THEM" CUE

The next game to play involving the keys is "Find them." Even if your dog is great at this game you should start at an easy stage and introduce the concept of "Find the keys." He should catch on quite quickly which will allow you to move on to discreetly hiding your keys and asking him to "Find the keys" a short while later. Leave them with a couple of other items so that he has to actively choose the keys in preference to the other things. If he makes a mistake, don't tell him off — just encourage him to keep looking for the keys. Reward the correct choice.

### PRACTICING WHILE OUT WALKING AND EVENTUALLY WITHOUT A "FIND THE KEYS" COMMAND

Practice "accidentally" dropping your keys as you walk with your dog. As they hit the ground encourage him to retrieve them for you. Remember to praise him and offer him a treat or even a game with his own toy as a reward.

The test is to drop your keys without asking your dog to retrieve and see how he responds. If he picks them up and returns them to you, make sure you reward him with a jackpot prize to show him that this is one of the best games around. This will encourage him to pay attention if you genuinely do drop your keys.

**TIP** Remember that if you are a little messy and tend to leave your keys lying around, you should be prepared to praise and reward your dog for "finding" them and returning them to you, even if you haven't really lost them. If you ignore him or tell him off, he won't bother the next time when you are genuinely looking for them.

**2** Getting him excited about this stage is important so that he develops a strong motivation to find them later on. He will probably play about with the keys at first so make sure that you have removed any fragile key-ring charms and that the set can't be accidentally swallowed.

# THE CANINE CLEANER

Most of us dream of having some help around the home. While there is no getting out of doing the vacuuming and dusting, your dog may be able to help you by putting the garbage into the bin.

| | INTERACTIVE GAME<br>Dog and Owner |
|---|---|
| **LOCATION** | A room of your choice. |
| **LEVEL OF DIFFICULTY** | ☆ ☆ ☆<br>**Good brain workout**<br>The "Retrieve" and "Tidy Toys" games will help. |
| **PROPS** | Empty plastic bottles or drinks cans, a bin that is low enough for your dog to easily reach into, treats. |

Once you can get your dog to retrieve reliably you can start this game. You will need to select items that your dog is happy to pick up. However, food wrappers are not a good idea since he is likely to become distracted and take them off to lick or chew. Empty plastic bottles or drink cans are safer although you must always be careful to check that they don't have any sharp edges. Spend time making sure that your dog is comfortable picking up the garbage items.

**IN THE BIN PLEASE**

**1** Place some garbage on the floor in front of the bin. Sit on the floor or on a chair with the bin in front of you. Ask your dog to retrieve one item.

**2** Encourage your dog to approach the bin by using an enthusiastic voice and holding out your hand into which he should return the item. At first he might drop it on the other side of the bin but don't worry since you can shape this into the action you want over the following sessions. Keep practicing and encouraging him to return the item directly to you.

**3** Your aim is to teach him to come close so that he is standing with his head over the bin before you take the item from him. Then praise him and offer your reward.

**4** The next stage involves you asking him to "Leave" or "Drop" the item once his head is over the bin. The garbage should drop and land in the bin. You can praise your dog and offer big rewards for this.

# TIDY TOYS

This game can also be adapted to teach your dog how to "Tidy His Toys." Teach him to pick up his toys and put them in his toy box. If your dog becomes distracted by the toy he is picking up, just stay calm. Don't try to chase after him as this will create more problems. Wait until the initial excitement is over and ask him to "Fetch it" again. If he continues to be too excited, then you should begin the game again later. Put the first toy away and pick another that he will retrieve back to you. Make sure that your rewards are enticing enough. As his performance improves, he can try again with the more exciting toys.

**TOYS IN THE BOX PLEASE**

**1** Start by practicing your retrieve in the room where you will teach your "Tidy Toys" command. Place the toy box in front of you. Throw the toy and hold your hands out over the box for him to drop the toy into them. Praise your dog for bringing the toy to you when called.

*That's the way! Praise your dog warmly when he drops the toy.*

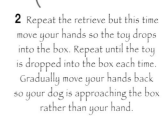

**2** Repeat the retrieve but this time move your hands so the toy drops into the box. Repeat until the toy is dropped into the box each time. Gradually move your hands back so your dog is approaching the box rather than your hand.

**KEEP PRACTICING**

Keep practicing until he can easily approach and drop the item into the bin (left). You can start to introduce a verbal command for this game such as "Bin it." Say this just as your dog drops the item into the bin and then, once he has made the association, you can say it earlier and earlier in the game until eventually you can point to the rubbish on the floor and say "Bin it."

**TIP** Some dogs will try to jump up at the bin and may pull it over. Either choose a different bin that your dog doesn't have to jump up to reach or place a weight in the bottom so it is less likely to topple over onto him.

# GAMES FOR SMALL AREAS

Some owners worry that their homes don't provide enough space for their dogs to play. This is not actually the case as many great brain games involve no special equipment and only require more focused actions. The games described in this chapter can also be played by dogs in larger areas. You may also want to look at chapter 8 on Verbal Brain Games to discover some extra challenges.

**NOSE TOUCH**
The easiest target is probably your hand since it involves no props and since most dogs will naturally approach their owners' hands.

## TARGETING TASKS

Teaching your dog to target or "touch" a specific item makes many other games and training tasks much easier. Clicker trainers use a lot of targeting but even if you aren't using a clicker, you can get the same results as long as the timing of your praise and rewards is accurate. Targeting can involve your dog using different parts of his body to touch an item of your choice. You may teach him to use any body part but most commonly we focus on the nose, paw, flank, chin or forehead. When you first begin, I recommend that you stick to one type of touch at a time so that you don't confuse him.

| INTERACTIVE GAME | |
|---|---|
| **Dog and Owner** | |
| **LOCATION** | Any room where your dog is comfortable. |
| **LEVEL OF DIFFICULTY** | ☆ to ☆☆☆ <br> **Easy to moderately brainy** |
| **PROPS** | Cardboard or Post-it note to create the target marker, treats. |

Practice asking your dog to "Touch" your hand while you are in different places and with varied distractions about you.

A nose touch is simple to teach. Begin by holding a treat in your closed fist. Hold it out and allow your dog to approach.

**TIP** Keep practicing until you can move your hand into different positions — to the left, to the right, in front of you, behind you, raised up and held down low. Your dog should begin to link the word "Touch" with the action.

As soon as his nose touches your hand praise and release the treat (if you are using a clicker, click when he touches your hand). Repeat a couple of times. When your dog is touching your hand very reliably you can introduce your verbal cue, "Touch."

### TOUCHING AN EMPTY HAND

The next stage is to then put your hand out without holding a treat. Your dog has learned to expect a reward so will probably go forwards and nose at your hand. At the moment his nose touches your hand say "Touch, good dog!," click if you are using a clicker, and give him a treat from your other hand.

### KEEP IT FOCUSED

If he tries to touch your hand without being asked to, you should ignore him. Later on when attempting other games involving touching, if you haven't practiced your touch for a while you should go back to some easy hand touches to remind your dog what you are expecting him to do.

# TARGET MARKING

Once your dog can reliably target your hand, you may want to refocus his attention onto a marker that can then be positioned away from your hand. An easy marker to use is a sticky Post-it note while a stiffer piece of card may provide a more robust target marker.
Essentially you are aiming to transfer the nose-touch response onto another physical object which can then be set in different places around your training area.

### POST-IT NOTE MARKER

**1** You can choose to hold this in your hand or you may prefer to attach it to your hand using the sticky edge of the Post-it, or with some double-sided craft tape. Hold out your hand in the same way as in the "Touch" game but use another verbal cue since this is a different task.

| | |
|---|---|
| | **INTERACTIVE GAME**<br>**Dog and Owner** |
| **LOCATION** | Any room where your dog is comfortable. |
| **LEVEL OF DIFFICULTY** | ☆ to ☆☆☆<br>**Easy to moderately brainy** |
| **PROPS** | Cardboard or Post-it note to create the target marker, treats. |

**2** Choose a cue such as "Nose" to act as your signal for this game when the time comes to introduce it. The main difference is that now he will actually be contacting the marker rather than your hand. Immediately reward him as he touches it.

#### KEEP PRACTICING

Keep practicing so that he is fully comfortable touching the marker. Be very accurate and only praise him if his nose is actually touching the marker. You can then introduce your cue word while you practice. To transfer the command word to your new activity, you say the new cue first followed immediately by the old one. So for this game you would begin by saying "Nose-touch." Say this each time until your dog anticipates the action when he hears the first word, "Nose."

#### PRACTICAL APPLICATIONS

Your dog can use his nose to play many games such as "Close the door," or even to turn on light switches. Be imaginative and you will probably find many things your dog can do with this lesson.

# TRANSFERRING THE MARKER

Your next step will be to transfer the marker onto another vertical surface. Hold it by your fingers and encourage him to touch it with his nose. Very gradually move its position so that it is stuck against a wall or a door, or some other vertical surface that is remote from your hand, such as the agility course cone illustrated here.

☆ ☆ ☆ **Good brain workout**

### VERTICAL MARKERS

**1** Every time your dog touches the marker say "Nose!" and "Good" or click and offer praise and rewards.

### HORIZONTAL MARKERS

**1** For horizontal markers you should gradually lower the marker in your hand and stick it to the floor. Withdraw your hand over the next few sessions so that your dog is focusing entirely on the marker.

**2** Over the next few sessions withdraw your hand so your dog is just targeting on the marker. If you practice enough, your dog should be able to go and touch a variety of items wherever the marker is positioned.

### PRACTICAL APPLICATIONS

Targeting your dog to your hand allows you to easily teach many other actions including doggy dancing and close heelwork. Next time you watch a professional performance try to spot what the dog has been taught to "target."

**2** This dog is now nose-touching the Post-it marker on the floor rather than the hand. Build up your dog's ability by moving him away from the marker. Wait until he is trying to pull back towards it before you release him while telling him to "Nose."

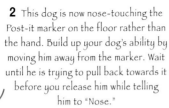

This dog is beautifully targeted on his owner's hand. This skill is important for competitive disciplines like heelwork.

# FOOT TOUCH

Some dogs are more inclined to use their paws than others and these will pick up the foot touch very quickly. You will require a new target marker so your dog doesn't become confused. Use something tough enough to withstand your dog standing on it or swiping it with his paw. Plastic lids are commonly used, as are squares of carpet or other material. Place your new marker on the floor. At first you should reward

**TRAINING A FOOT TOUCH**
Progress the training in the same way as the nose touch and when your dog is reliably going out to touch the target with his paw you should introduce your chosen verbal cue: "Press" or "Toes" perhaps.

# PUSH THE DOOR CLOSED

Fix your dog's marker (**1**) to the inside of the closed door (**2**). Send him to touch the marker making sure you offer praise at exactly the moment he touches the door.

| | INTERACTIVE GAME |
|---|---|
| | Dog and Owner |
| **LOCATION** | Inside your home. |
| **LEVEL OF DIFFICULTY** | ☆ ☆ ☆ **Good brain workout** Reliable "Touch" to a vertical marker needed. |
| **PROPS** | Internal door that pushes closed, target marker, tape to fix marker to door, door stop, treats. |

Open the door a little for the next stage so your dog gets used to approaching the door while the marker is at a different angle. Prevent it from moving and putting him off by placing a door-stop behind it. Practice sending your dog to touch the

marker with the door opened to different degrees.

You are now ready to add in your new verbal cue. Your cue to touch the marker was "Toes" so at first this will have to be part of the new cue. If you choose a sound that is very similar to the original cue (like "Close"), this should be a very easy transition to make although your initial command will sound rather comical. Begin by saying both words together, "Close-Toes!" so your dog pays attention to the first word you say. Eventually you will be able to say just "Close" and he will know what is meant.

When you feel that your dog is pushing on the marker confidently, you can start to encourage him to actually push the

1

**UP HIGHER**
You can also teach a foot
touch against a raised object
or a vertical surface.

your dog for going to investigate it, especially if he touches it with his foot. Some dogs are more likely to use their paws if you hide a little piece of food under the marker. If you do this, you will have to focus on clicking and/or praising the moment his paw touches the marker so he doesn't become fixated on trying to overturn it.

door closed (**3**). Remove the door-stop and start with the door left open just a few centimeters so that he has only a little way to push it to achieve success. Build up his ability to push the door closed slowly and always make it rewarding for him.

**TIP** Once your dog is reliably touching the marker you can choose to begin to reduce its size. Very gradually cut the marker down and practice the game at each stage. Eventually you may just be left with a small dot, or even no marker at all.

# INDOOR AGILITY

Dogs without much access to their own outdoor space can still enjoy some of the fun of an obstacle course. Of course you will have to be prepared for an excited dog in your house. An indoor agility course is more about precision and control than charging madly around, however, so it may serve as a distraction for an otherwise too-bouncy dog.

The first key to putting your dog around any obstacle course is to make sure that he is comfortable with every stage individually. You can then link them together one by one to create the final course.

Think about your space and what your dog could be taught to do there. Your choice will be influenced by the type of dog you own.

Think about the layout of your room. Decide on a sensible route for your dog's obstacle course. Remember that he will need room to jump and land and the course should not take him too close to fragile items.

Teach each part of the course separately and then choose two elements that will naturally come together

| | INTERACTIVE GAME |
|---|---|
| | Dog and Owner |
| **LOCATION** | Any room where your dog is comfortable. |
| **LEVEL OF DIFFICULTY** | ☆ ☆ ☆ **Good brain workout** |
| **PROPS** | Furniture and common household items, treats. Must be on suitable flooring if you are encouraging jumping. May include many brain games from this book. |

# PLAY BOX

A basic cardboard box filled with some scrunched-up paper can really provide an exciting game

opportunity for a dog. It's particularly exciting for adventurous puppies. What you actually do with your play box really depends on your dog's own tendencies. It might be an object in your obstacle course or could contain a special prize that your dog is searching for.

| | SOLO GAME |
|---|---|
| | Dog alone |
| **LOCATION** | Any room where your dog is comfortable. |
| **LEVEL OF DIFFICULTY** | ☆ ☆ **Moderate brain tester** |
| **PROPS** | A cardboard box, shredded paper, toys, treats. |

on your route and begin practicing them both. Since your dog knows each part already, this won't take long to achieve. Keep your rewards for when he has successfully completed both parts. Slowly add on more obstacles and practice until your dog is comfortable with his whole performance.

So that your dog does not just charge around uncontrollably, you can include control points where he has to perform a "Down" or a "Sit" in one place for a count of five before you release him to approach the next obstacle.

**INSIDE OBSTACLE IDEAS INCLUDE:**
Weaving around chair or table legs.
Crawling under a chair, table or broom handle.
Running through a tunnel made from a blanket draped over a table, or a child's play tunnel.
Doing a "Down" on a mat or on a chair.
Jumping on a chair.
Jumping over a mini-jump.

**TIP** Use dry treats so that the paper itself doesn't absorb the flavor and so become interesting for your dog to eat.

**2** Begin with just a little shredded paper at first and add more as your dog gets the hang of the game. Throw some favorite treats inside the box or hide his favorite toy in there.

**1** If you don't mind a little papery mess, you can add some extra interest in the form of shredded paper inside the box. Select paper that is soft and without toxic ink which could also stain your dog's coat.

**3** Scattering a handful of kibble pieces should encourage him to forage and play around inside his play box for an enjoyable while.

# GAMES FOR THE GARDEN

Many dogs spend a great deal of time relaxing in their gardens. However, we often forget that this area is ideal for playing games. Take advantage of this space while keeping your dog busy. He will be happier as a result and will develop fewer unwanted habits too.

## DIGGING FOR TREASURE

Some dogs have an insatiable urge to dig, which can be devastating to your garden. Redirecting this activity is usually much easier than stopping it completely so it can pay to create a special area where your dog can freely dig in search of buried treasure.

Position your sandpit in a convenient place in your garden. Its size will depend upon your dog, but it should be deep enough for him to be able to dig down at least a few inches and for you to easily bury biscuits and toys.

Wooden crates are cheap options but try to avoid wood that splinters easily. Plastic containers are convenient but may get water-logged if they are left uncovered in the rain.

Show your dog a toy that he really likes to play with. Tease him with it and then partially bury it in the sandpit.

| SOLO GAME | |
|---|---|
| **Dog alone** | |
| **LOCATION** | In your garden or secure outdoor area. |
| **LEVEL OF DIFFICULTY** | ☆ ☆ **Moderate brain tester** |
| **PROPS** | Large deep, wooden crate or a child's plastic sandpit filled with clean, fine sand. Rubber toys to bury and large dog biscuits. |

> **TIP** Remember to cover the sandpit while it is not in use since neighborhood cats may be tempted to use it as a toilet. Remember to uncover it when your dog is outside playing though. Children should not use this sandpit unless they are playing with your dog in it.

# FROZEN POPSICLES

Help your dog to cool off on hot days by making him a "Frozen Popsicle" to play with. These are reasonably quick to prepare and you can vary the flavor to suit your dog's tastes. Choose between small ice-cube-sized treats for small dogs or larger versions which will last longer and help to cool down your dog on the hottest of days.

To make your iced lolly you can be quite creative. Natural stock or low-salt gravy cubes are popular choices although it is also possible to use lactose-free milk. Mix your choice in a jug with plenty of water. The solution does not need to be very strong to interest your dog.

A simple popsicle can be made by dropping treats or peanut butter balls into the ice-cube holder or larger container which is then topped up with the solution you have prepared in the jug. Then freeze them until they are solid.

### FIND THE BURIED TREASURE

Encourage your dog to approach the sandpit to pull out the toy. When he does, praise him and encourage him to play. Repeat this part a few times to make sure that he has understood the idea of the game. As he progresses you should bury the toy a little deeper. Add extra excitement by placing dog biscuits in the sand for him to find while he digs. Toys that can be buried in the sand without damage include all the rubber and plastic varieties although on dry days any toy can be used.

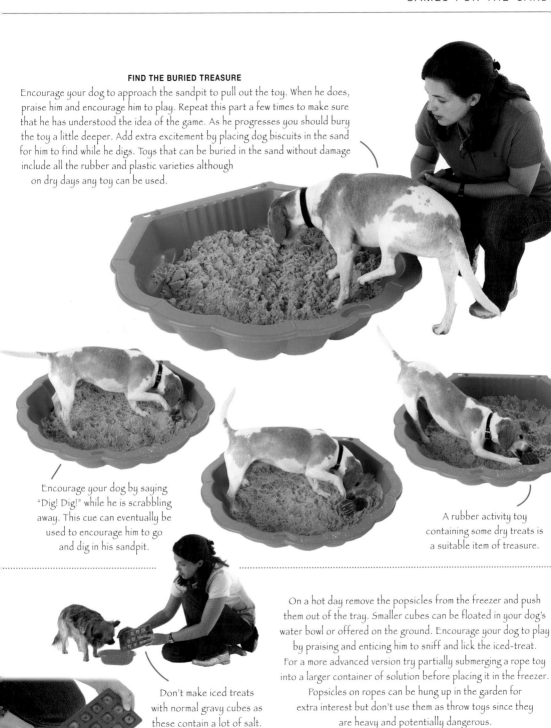

Encourage your dog by saying "Dig! Dig!" while he is scrabbling away. This cue can eventually be used to encourage him to go and dig in his sandpit.

A rubber activity toy containing some dry treats is a suitable item of treasure.

Don't make iced treats with normal gravy cubes as these contain a lot of salt.

On a hot day remove the popsicles from the freezer and push them out of the tray. Smaller cubes can be floated in your dog's water bowl or offered on the ground. Encourage your dog to play by praising and enticing him to sniff and lick the iced-treat. For a more advanced version try partially submerging a rope toy into a larger container of solution before placing it in the freezer. Popsicles on ropes can be hung up in the garden for extra interest but don't use them as throw toys since they are heavy and potentially dangerous.

# TOY BUNGEE

When thinking of ways to enrich your dog's environment, it pays to think about it from all angles. While toys on the floor provide lots of fun, hanging toys can provide your dog with even more of a challenge.

Loop a bungee rope (ideally a length of elasticized cord which can stretch and rebound a little) over your clothes-line so

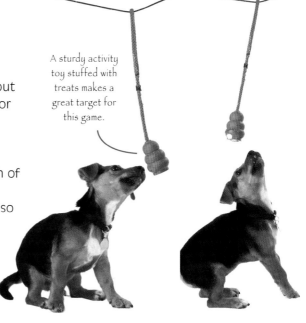

A sturdy activity toy stuffed with treats makes a great target for this game.

| | SOLO GAME | 
|---|---|
| | **Dog alone** |
| **LOCATION** | Area with a strong clothes-line. |
| **LEVEL OF DIFFICULTY** | ☆ ☆ **Moderate brain tester** |
| **PROPS** | Activity toy on a rope, bungee rope or stretchy lead. |

When your dog grabs the toy you should praise and encourage him. If he has to stretch up to reach the toy or pulls at it, the bungee rope will result in a "bounce" when he lets go. This will entice your dog to go after the toy again and will result in treats dropping out.

# SKIPPING

This game is easiest with agile, smaller dogs that can easily jump on cue. It is not a good game for very heavy or young dogs. It's easiest to teach your dog to jump over the rope on his own although if you are feeling energetic and own a fit dog, you may want to learn to skip together.

If you don't have a helper, then you should tie one end of the skipping rope to a static object, such as a fence post. You can then turn the rope from the other end with your dog in the middle.

The skipping game begins very slowly.

Initially you should teach him to jump over the rope while it is lying still in front of him. Once he can jump well, move on to the next step.

| | INTERACTIVE GAME |
|---|---|
| | **Dog and Owner** |
| **LOCATION** | In an open area. |
| **LEVEL OF DIFFICULTY** | ☆ ☆ ☆ ☆ ☆ <br> **A proper brainteaser** <br> Teach your dog to "Jump Over" first. |
| **PROPS** | Skipping rope and treats. A helper may be useful. |

*As you raise the height of the toy, your dog will have to work harder for the rewards.*

*You can hang different toys from the line for variety or even from a sturdy tree or fence.*

that it can move freely along the line when pulled. Make sure that the line to which you attach the toy is strong enough to sustain the pressure of your dog's tugging and pulling at it. Tie your toy securely to the bungee rope. (Remember to stuff activity toys with tidbits of food and treats before hanging them up.)

The height of the dangling toy will depend on the size of your dog. It should not be too high as this will make it difficult for him to get involved. Begin with it at just above head height and then move it progressively higher as your dog begins to get the hang of it.

**TIP** Avoid filling the activity toy with any foodstuff that could attract wasps or bees. Once your dog has finished playing, take the toy down as it could attract wildlife and insects, or be damaged by the elements if it is left hanging outside for too long.

Begin to introduce movement to the rope. Gently sway it back and forth in front of your dog keeping it low to the ground. Encourage him to "Jump" it as it moves towards him. Take care not to overwhelm him with too much movement at once. This stage often takes lots of practice to ensure your dog is not hesitating at all.

**TIP** If you decide to try skipping along with your dog, you should take extreme care not to jump and land on your dog's paws.

### GET IN THE SWING

*Gradually increase the rope's arc of movement. Praise him for successfully jumping over the rope. The first stages will be slow, but the more you practice the quicker your dog will begin to learn to anticipate the jump each time. Take care never to swing the rope into your dog's legs. Be patient and don't rush.*

# CREATING AN OUTDOOR OBSTACLE COURSE

Owners of more active dogs will probably benefit from creating activities within their own gardens. You can make a small course consisting of perhaps just two activities or make use of more space with some of the suggestions that follow in this section. If you really enjoy this type of activity, you can purchase home agility kits, although you may also benefit from attending your local agility group class.

## JUMPING HOOPS

Begin by holding your hoop vertically so that the lower part is touching the ground. Hold it with one hand and hold a treat in the other.

**SINGLE HOOP**
**1** Begin to train this game by luring your dog through a hoop resting on the ground.

**TWO HOOPS**
**4** An extension to this game is to ask a family member or friend to hold another hoop for you so that your dog can land and jump again.

| | INTERACTIVE GAME Dog and Owner |
|---|---|
| **LOCATION** | Open area with a suitable surface for landing on. |
| **LEVEL OF DIFFICULTY** | ☆☆ Moderate brain tester |
| **PROPS** | A plastic hoop sized to suit dog and treats or toy. |

Lure your dog through the hoop with the treat (**1**). As he goes through praise him and give him the reward. Practice with the hoop on the floor until your dog is very comfortable going through it even when you move to a slightly different location.

As he gets confident at going through the hoop, you can add in a cue word such as "Jump." Actual jumping will require a little more space so ensure that your dog has a direct run-up and landing area.

**2** Now hold the hoop a little way off the floor. Don't be tempted to hold the hoop too high to begin with as this could be dangerous and off-putting for your dog.

**3** As your dog improves you can slowly raise the hoop a bit at a time to encourage him to jump higher. Don't raise it too high too quickly. Build up your dog's jumping skills slowly.

**5** A double jump is extra fun. As this involves two take-offs and two landings, it is very important to make sure that the surface is not slippery. On polished floors, use a long mat or length of carpet.

**MINI-HOOPS FOR SMALL DOGS**

If you own a very tiny dog then you can be a little more imaginative when playing Jumping Hoops. An old tennis racquet with the strings removed can make a great "hoop" to jump through. If you own a small to medium dog, you may like to create a hoop with your arms and encourage your dog to jump through.

**TIP** You may want to buy or make your own free-standing hoop jump. Dog agility equipment suppliers are a good place to begin your search. The benefit of this type of equipment is that you can include it in a series of activities making up your own home-agility routine.

# TUNNEL DASH

The tunnel dash is always a fun addition to an obstacle course. Fabric tunnels are available specifically for dogs although there are also some good quality children's ones on the market.

It is possible to improvise one using six short poles inserted in pairs into the ground at equal distances apart.

Throw an old blanket over them and it should create a temporary tunnel for you to begin training (this isn't as good, however, as the dog may exit from under the blanket at the side).

Make sure that the play tunnel cannot roll while your dog is inside by anchoring it to the ground or placing restraining objects on either side. Allow your dog time to get used to the tunnel and encourage him to investigate it in his own time.

Tease him with a treat and then throw a few inside the tunnel. He should step inside to reach the food. Move around to the exit and encourage him to run all the way

| | **INTERACTIVE GAME** Dog and Owner | |
|---|---|---|
| **LOCATION** | Area with space for a tunnel. | |
| **LEVEL OF DIFFICULTY** | ☆ Easy brain exercise | |
| **PROPS** | Doggy tunnel or children's play tunnel and treats or toys. | |

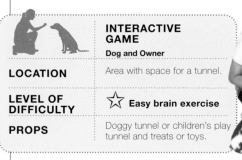

# ZIGZAGGING

The aim of this game is for your dog to weave in a zigzag action in and out between the objects. In agility competitions this is done with poles but at home you can start with any number of different items. Plastic cones or pots are a

simple way to create a course and garden canes are excellent if you are on a lawn.

Begin by placing two or three or more cones in a straight line allowing plenty of space in between for your dog to walk easily between them. If your dog generally responds warily to new items, then you should allow him to sniff and explore the equipment before you begin.

Using a treat or a toy as a reward, lure your dog to walk between the first two cones. Praise him as he does. Continue luring him back through the next two cones and reward him. It's a simple game but the aim is to get your dog zigzagging between the cones as quickly as possible.

| | **INTERACTIVE GAME** Dog and Owner | |
|---|---|---|
| **LOCATION** | Any open area with space for three or more poles. | |
| **LEVEL OF DIFFICULTY** | ☆ Easy brain exercise | |
| **PROPS** | Select from: garden canes, weave poles, plastic cones or upturned plant pots. Treats. | |

### STEP THIS WAY

Ready-made tunnels can be compressed down into a hoop shape. Nervous dogs may find this less challenging to start with.

With encouragement, your dog should soon be charging through the full length.

**TIP** If your dog appears very cautious, it can help to concertina the tunnel, as if you are packing it away. Practice getting your dog to step though the "hoop" it makes. Very gradually open it up so that your dog only has to move through a very short tunnel at first.

through. It can help to have a helper hold your dog at one end of the tunnel while you go to the other. Call him through and praise him for responding. Many dogs love to chase a toy through the tunnel for extra fun.

When your dog is racing through the tunnel, you can add in your cue word, such as "Through," to link the action to a verbal cue.

**SAFETY TIP** If you are using canes or poles, ensure that you place plastic caps or rubber tips on the ends so that you don't risk damaging an eye with a cane when you bend over to reward your dog.

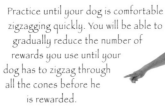

### TIGHTENING UP THE COURSE

Once he is moving between the cones comfortably, you may want to bring them a little closer together. The distance between the cones must be in proportion to your dog's physical size and shape.

Practice until your dog is comfortable zigzagging quickly. You will be able to gradually reduce the number of rewards you use until your dog has to zigzag through all the cones before he is rewarded.

# GAMES TO PLAY WHILE OUT AND ABOUT

Taking your dog out is not just about walking him. For many dogs a walk becomes less about interacting with their owners and more about finding exciting things to do. While indulging a little of this behavior is fine, losing your dog's attention completely is a real problem and makes maintaining full control over him harder. If he is allowed to find fun distractions that don't involve you, then he'll be less inclined to stay close and respond to your calls. Instead, use your walking time to both exercise his body and brain. You'll have fun together and he'll have less time to discover bad habits.

As the toy winds back towards you, dogs will think the chase is on.

**AN EXTENDING LEAD**
These items, sometimes called flexi-leads, consist of a length of strong lead that rolls up onto a reel that is spring-loaded. The lead runs out against the torsion of the spring and can be locked into place by the use of a button control.

## EXTENDABLE EXCITEMENT

Many dog owners own pieces of equipment that they no longer use. This game suggests a use for an extendable lead that can help you to encourage your dog to play near you, to run towards you, and to learn that you are the provider of unlimited fun! The lead may be one you still use, or one that's sitting unused in your cupboard. Either way, as long as the retracting button still works, you can play this game.

| | **INTERACTIVE GAME** |
|---|---|
| | Dog and Owner |
| **LOCATION** | In any safe, open area. |
| **LEVEL OF DIFFICULTY** | ☆ ☆ **Moderate brain tester** |
| **PROPS** | An extendable lead, treats and a toy. |

### FOLLOW THAT TOY!

**1** Dogs often love to chase small things moving quickly along the ground. This game tries to harness those instincts into a safe and fulfilling activity. While your dog is otherwise distracted on a walk, attach a small, soft toy to the end of the flexi-lead. Casually drop the toy and begin to feed out the lead as you continue walking. Use the "lock" button to stop it reeling in.

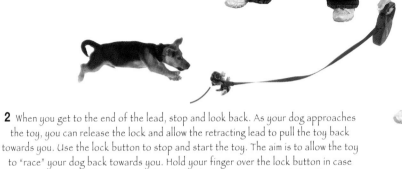

**2** When you get to the end of the lead, stop and look back. As your dog approaches the toy, you can release the lock and allow the retracting lead to pull the toy back towards you. Use the lock button to stop and start the toy. The aim is to allow the toy to "race" your dog back towards you. Hold your finger over the lock button in case your dog accidentally gets tangled in the lead. This game is particularly effective when the toy is whizzing through leaves or longer grasses.

The lead winds back into this plastic handle.

**TIP** Use lighter toys, such as large feathers or strips of furry material, for smaller dogs and for faster returns.

### OTHER VARIATIONS

For more advanced playing options you can bend the lead around a tree to create an L shape or even a U shape. Pick one with smooth bark at the base or you might find the toy or lead becomes snagged. You will now find that your toy will initially move away from you before turning and zooming back towards you once it has rounded the tree. This is a great lesson for dogs that do run off while on walks. They can have fun but the ultimate goal is to turn and rush back to their owner for the rewards they know await them.

# SKATER DOG

This is an excellent game that challenges both you and your dog. It also results in a great party piece. But please remember: safety is imperative at all times and you should never encourage your dog to do anything he is not comfortable with. Although this is ultimately a game for outdoors, you can begin teaching this inside on a rug or carpet since movement is one of the last parts to add to the game. When you do choose to move locations, remember to take the game back a few stages to encourage your dog with easier steps again.

| | INTERACTIVE GAME |
|---|---|
| | **Dog and Owner** |
| **LOCATION** | On a flat surface. |
| **LEVEL OF DIFFICULTY** | ☆☆☆☆ **Advanced brain game** |
| **PROPS** | A skateboard, treats, two bricks or heavy books, marker for foot touch. |

Take the first stages quite slowly — the skateboard will be unfamiliar.

**GETTING YOUR DOG UP ON THE BOARD**

**1** Park your skateboard between two heavy bricks or books positioned at the front and back so that it can't move when your dog touches it. Spend time luring your dog up onto the skateboard until he is comfortable putting both his front feet there. Teach him to place his feet near the center of the skateboard since it will tip up if he puts his weight at the back end.

**WAVE TO THE CROWD**
Some dogs get to feel so at home on a skateboard that they can be taught to do extra tricks while still up on the board.

**BE A SYMPATHETIC TEACHER**
If your dog is confident enough, he should eventually be able to put all four paws on it and move forward. Don't rush this, however, and be understanding if your dog remains apprehensive of this unfamiliar object. It is not fair to keep coaxing an animal to perform a game that makes him anxious.

**PRACTICE MAKES PERFECT**
Once a dog has become accustomed to the initial feeling of instability that he will experience as the board rolls forward, he may become assured enough to hop on as the board moves.

**2** You can then begin to move the front brick forwards by a few centimeters so that the skateboard will move very slightly. Prepare yourself with some high-value treats and offer these as soon as your dog moves the board a fraction.

Have some favorite treats ready to hand as rewards.

**3** When your dog is comfortable with the slight movement, you can begin to move the bricks a little farther away. Gradually increasing the distance the board moves is important so your dog doesn't become frightened. Reward him for each successful attempt.

**4** Your cue for this game can be "Skate." Say this just as your dog steps onto the skateboard. Keep practicing until he has made a solid association between the word and the action. Eventually, you will be able to ask your dog to "Skate" and he will go over to his board and hop on.

Slowly the brick end-stops can be discarded.

**TIP** Never play this game on a steep hill or near traffic. The ground surface does not need to be perfectly flat and smooth since it's better for your dog if the board moves quite slowly.

# HIDE AND SEEK

Hide and Seek is a great game that encourages your dog to pay attention to you on walks. He learns that searching for you and finding you is great fun. It can also distract him from wandering off and doing as he pleases. Always choose an area away from roads, railways or other dangers.

| | **INTERACTIVE GAME** |
|---|---|
| | Dog and Owner |
| **LOCATION** | In a safe outdoor area. |
| **LEVEL OF DIFFICULTY** | ☆ ☆ ☆ **Good brain workout** A reliable "Come" should be taught so you can let your dog off lead safely. |
| **PROPS** | Treats or a toy. |

**RUN AND HIDE**

**1** When your dog is not paying any attention, perhaps when distracted by a smell or just trotting ahead of you, you should slip behind a tree or a bush that's close to your path.

# CARRY IT

Wouldn't it be lovely to have a dog that could help us carry things along? Some dogs are naturals at the Carry It game while others need more training. Overall, however, this is a fun game to play which can serve a useful purpose too.

| | **INTERACTIVE GAME** |
|---|---|
| | Dog and Owner |
| **LOCATION** | Along your normal walking route. |
| **LEVEL OF DIFFICULTY** | ☆ ☆ ☆ **Good brain workout** Teach a reliable "Retrieve." |
| **PROPS** | A toy or other item you wish your dog to carry. |

**MAKE A CHOICE**

Decide what you would like your dog to carry. Many owners like their dogs to carry their toy or a newspaper.

**1** Encourage your dog to hold the item in his mouth. Tease him with it and get him a little excited. He is likely to then try to pick the item up when you throw it on the floor. As he returns to you, praise him and walk back a few paces so that he has to walk with you before you take the item from him and offer the reward.

**2** Wait a moment and then call out to your dog. Dogs can easily spot movement so keep very still. Position yourself so that you can peep round the tree to see what your dog is doing and to make sure he is safe. If he has stopped and is looking back but is not sure of what to do, call out again in a really excited voice.

**3** As he rushes to find you, help by calling out a few times. When he does find you, praise him and even have a good game with his toy. When you get really good, your dog will know to come looking for you after just one call. He will also keep a closer eye on you since he'll think his silly human tends to get lost on walks!

**TIP** This game can be a little embarrassing if another dog walker passes by and finds you hiding behind a tree! Don't worry though, your dog will soon appear and all will become clear. To save your blushes, play this game in quieter areas.

**2** Gradually encourage your dog to take the item and to carry it a little farther while he walks along with you before you stop and praise him. Take the item away for a short time and then try again. As he walks along holding the item give your cue phrase "Carry it" and praise him often.

**3** Build up duration slowly until your dog will happily carry the item alongside you. Remember, though, that dogs will often drop what they are carrying when they meet another dog or detect a really good smell along the path. It will take practice and a strong instinct for this never to happen. So it pays to practice this with something like a dog toy first. Teach him to "Find it" so he can retrace his steps to pick up any dropped items easily.

Using tasty treats as rewards can make a dog's mouth slobbery, so try to reward with play, praise and basic, dry treats.

# NATURE'S OBSTACLE COURSE

There are many opportunities to use up your dog's energy through encouraging physical exertion, balance and coordination while out on walks. Every location is different but you can be imaginative and create your own fun on your regular walks. Before you ask your dog to "Jump" on or off anything, check that it is safe to do so. There may be broken glass, steep drops, sharp branches or hard surfaces that may cause injury to your dog.

**BELOW** Jumping over streams does not come much more athletic than this!

| INTERACTIVE GAME | |
|---|---|
| Dog and Owner | |
| **LOCATION** | On your walk. |
| **LEVEL OF DIFFICULTY** | ☆ ☆ ☆ **Good brain workout** Try teaching indoor and garden obstacle course maneuvers first. |
| **PROPS** | Varies depending on your area. Treats. |

**EXAMPLES OF ACTIVITIES:**
- Jumping over fallen trees.
- Walking along fallen tree trunks.
- Weaving between trees or fence posts.
- Going under trunks or branches.
- Jumping over small streams.

# EGG AND SPOON RACE

This traditional game provides lots of fun for owners and dogs of all levels of training. Your "egg" can be anything that you can balance on your spoon (though you should avoid small rubber balls).

**RULES OF THE GAME:**
- Dogs must not be pulled or dragged around at any point during the race.
- Praise and reward the dogs for good behavior.
- Holding the "egg" to the spoon with a thumb is classed as cheating!
- If the dog picks up the egg, you should swap it for a treat.

| INTERACTIVE GAME | |
|---|---|
| Several pairs of dogs/owners | |
| **LOCATION** | In your garden or local park |
| **LEVEL OF DIFFICULTY** | ☆ ☆ ☆ **Good brain workout** |
| **PROPS** | One soup spoon per person, boiled eggs/tennis balls/bean bags, poles or chairs and treats. |

**AGREE ON THE RULES BEFORE YOU START**
Decide on what form your game will take. The most common game involves all owners walking their dogs (on lead) together around a pre-agreed route. This will usually involve weaving around chairs or garden poles but can be as complex as you wish.

**1** Each owner should loop their dog's lead over one hand in which they will also hold a spoon. Everyone should take an "egg" and find their places at the starting line.

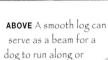

**MIX AND MATCH**
You can teach the individual activities as described in Chapters 4 and 6 covering indoor obstacle courses and garden games and adapt them for outdoor use.

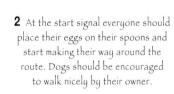

**ABOVE** A smooth log can serve as a beam for a dog to run along or a hurdle to jump over.

**2** At the start signal everyone should place their eggs on their spoons and start making their way around the route. Dogs should be encouraged to walk nicely by their owner.

**3** If you drop your "egg," you must stop, pick it up and restart the race from the drop point as quickly as possible. The winners are the first owner and dog pair who make it to the end line with their egg intact.

**TIP** Owners with highly trained dogs can make this game harder by creating a more complex course and by using uncooked eggs. If the egg breaks, you are eliminated.

Often, more haste means less speed.

# VERBAL BRAIN GAMES

The majority of canine communication is done via body language, unlike the case with humans who rely primarily on verbal interaction. Although the greater part of your dog training is done using both body and hand gestures, more advanced dogs can learn to respond to words only. This takes time to practice and lots of consistency and repetition. This may already be part of your formal obedience training but, if not, you may want to attempt the following games to increase your dog's response to verbal cues.

*Seduto – Sit*

Here the owner is starting to teach Italian to an Italian Greyhound.

| | INTERACTIVE GAME | |
|---|---|---|
| | **Dog and Owner** | |
| **LOCATION** | Anywhere. | |
| **LEVEL OF DIFFICULTY** | ☆☆☆ **Good brain workout** Teach your dog the actions and original words reliably first. | |
| **PROPS** | Treats and perhaps a foreign language phrase book. | |

**SPEAKING MANY TONGUES**
It's fun to tailor your verbal commands to reflect the origin of the breed of dog you own. Owners of Pekingese may need to allow for a little more research time, however!

*Platz*

# MULTILINGUAL TRICKS

*Seduto*

Imagine your friend's astonishment when they witness your dog responding to commands in another language. For extra effect you could teach the command words in the language of the country where your dog's breed originated. For example, your German Shepherd, French Bulldog or Italian Spinone can all learn some of their mother tongue. For those of us with dogs from English-speaking countries, remember that it never hurts to learn a second language!

*Giù – Down*

**TRAINING "DOWN" IN ITALIAN**
**1** Your dog should already have a really good response to the command you want to re-name. Pick one command at a time and be clear on the new cue word before you begin.

*Giù – Down*

**2** Introduce the new cue word immediately before saying the old one. In this way your dog will start to pay attention to the new word. Saying it afterwards doesn't work as well since your dog will be too busy following the original command to notice the new word.

*Attend*

*Giù*

*Dà la zampa*

**SOME EXAMPLES OF REPLACEMENT CUES**

| English | SIT | DOWN | PAW |
|---------|-----|------|-----|
| German | Sitz (nice easy one!) | Platz | Gib Pfötchen |
| French | Assis | Couche | Patte |
| Italian | Seduto | Giù | Dà la zampa |

**PRACTICE MAKES PERFECT**
Of course the word "zampa" (paw) in itself means nothing to the dog — he is merely learning a verbal cue to elicit the desired behavior.

Example: To re-train the "Down" in German, get your dog's attention and say: "Platz-Down" and reward him for getting it right. Repeat several times until he responds correctly when he hears "Platz."

# TOY IDENTITY PARADE

This game teaches your dog to identify and pick out a specific toy on request. If you have already introduced toys and taught your dog a word associated with each of them, then you can progress directly to this game. If you haven't spent much time doing this, then you need to go back and start now. While your dog is playing with a toy say its name, for example "Ball." If you are consistent, your dog will begin to associate that word with that toy.

**STARTING SIMPLE**
**1** This game relies on your dog being able to recognize the names for individual toys. Start with just one simple example, like a ball.

**BUILD UP THE SKILL**
Practice by mixing the toys you use and moving them around until your dog knows which one you are asking for by name.

| | INTERACTIVE GAME |
|---|---|
| | **Dog and Owner** |
| **LOCATION** | Anywhere free of distractions. |
| **LEVEL OF DIFFICULTY** | ☆ ☆ ☆ ☆ <br> **Advanced brain game** <br> Teach your dog names for his toys during play and retrieve games. |
| **PROPS** | Treats, selection of toys, board with eye-hooks, strong string. |

To improve your dog's ability to correctly identify each toy, you will need to test his ability to distinguish it from other toys. However, it is important that he can't actually pick up the other toys since he might find playing with those more exciting which will set you back.

A good way of working around this is to use a toy board made from a large square of plywood. Attach some curved eye-hooks to the board in various places

ensuring that they cannot hurt your dog at all. Tie a couple of other toys to the board using your string and the eye-hooks. The toy you are training your dog to pick out should be placed on the board but must not be attached to it. This means that when your dog goes to the board, he won't be able to pick up any toy other than the one you have asked for. This is setting him up for success.

**2** Ask your dog to pick up the toy and say its name — "Ball" — as part of the command. Practice this a few times to let the lesson really sink in.

**ADD SOME CHOICE TO THE BOARD**
Once your dog is confidently picking up the individual toy that you name, you can start to introduce a little more complexity to the game. Anchor a selection of toys to the hooks on the board, but leave your chosen one free to pick up.

The ball can still be picked up and brought to you.

**THE SELECTION GETS EVEN WIDER**
**1** Now the ball is one of six choices that appear on the board. Place it in position and ask your dog to pick up the "Ball." You want him to distinguish what the command word means.

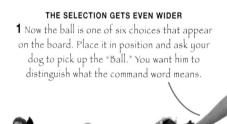

**TIP** Choose names for the toys that don't sound alike to make the distinction between them easier.

**2** If he picks up the ball, congratulate yourselves on a job well done. Once he has learned "Ball," begin with a different toy. Take your time and don't rush or your dog will get confused.

# TRAVELING GAMES

These days we travel with our pets more than ever. However, long journeys can be tedious for our dogs as well as for us. Break up the journey with time for exercise whenever possible and distract your dog during the journey by providing him with

activities to enjoy. Settling quietly in a hotel can also be difficult if your dog has spent the day traveling, so make sure you make time for a little mental stimulation to use up some of his extra energies.

These Traveling Games don't involve much extra equipment so you don't need to remember to pack things you wouldn't normally take with you on a journey with your dog. If you have previously taught some of the party games (Chapter 15), many of these can also be practiced while you are away. Make sure your dog is relaxed first and initially make the tricks easier to achieve since he is away from home in a new environment.

| | INTERACTIVE GAME |
|---|---|
| | **Solo Dog** |
| **LOCATION** | In the car crate or even when secured on the back seat. |
| **LEVEL OF DIFFICULTY** | ☆ **Easy brain exercise** |
| **PROPS** | Selection of activity toys, tub containing suitable food and treats, a protective seat cover. |

# CATCH THE TREAT

Not all dogs can coordinate themselves enough to catch a treat or a toy thrown towards them. This is something that you can teach and it encourages more precision and control over their movements. A dog that can catch is better prepared for other active outdoor games including playing with a Frisbee, or even competing in a rapid-fire activity like flyball (see Chapter 16).

Once your dog is catching the treat reliably, you can add in your cue word "Catch" just as you throw the treat. Practice in different places and with different things. Smaller treats are harder

and so more challenging. Toys can be thrown farther and move in different ways which will teach your dog more about being agile and coordinated.

| | INTERACTIVE GAME |
|---|---|
| | **Dog and Owner** |
| **LOCATION** | In your hotel room or even outside. |
| **LEVEL OF DIFFICULTY** | ☆ ☆ **Moderate brain tester** Teach "Leave it" or have a helper available. |
| **PROPS** | Treats (variety of sizes) or a toy. |

# IN-CAR ENTERTAINMENT

The great thing about many activity toys is that they can be easily transported and washed while you are traveling. They don't take up much space in the car and can provide your dog with a much needed distraction. Some can be left to roll around inside your travel crate while others, such as those with rope attachments, can be tied to the seatbelt or car crate to keep them in place. Take the opportunity to stuff the toy with new treats or food when you stop for a break and remember to offer your dog plenty of water as well.

**PACK AN INTERESTING TOY FOR THE JOURNEY**
Treat-filled activity toys are just the job to help a dog while away the hours during a long car journey. They can be easily refilled and washed clean at the end of the day.

**THROW IN A GENTLE ARC**
Stand facing your dog. Show him the treat you have in your hand. Throw the treat in an upwards arc towards your dog's head. Try to make this easy to catch at first. If he succeeds, make a fuss of him.

If he misses it, tell him to "Leave it" and pick the treat up from the floor. Ideally, he should not be allowed to eat it unless he catches it.

There are two things to consider about a miss:
1 **Overly keen?** Did your dog close his mouth too soon so the treat bounced off his nose?
2 **Too slow?** Did your dog open and close his mouth too late so the treat was already past his nose before he reacted?

You can adjust your position so that your dog has the best chance of catching the treat. If he is too fast, then you can step closer so the thrown treat arrives a little sooner. If your dog is too slow, then step back and throw from a little further away so that he has a little longer to react.

**TIP** Don't throw small balls to a large dog as they may become stuck in his throat.

113

# POKER FACE

Most dogs respond to a range of cues that we give them while we train. This is why they react so well to our hand signals and body movements as well as our verbal comments. It is hard to hide anything from our dogs as they are so used to "reading" us. This game aims to test your dog's understanding of the verbal command words you have taught him while removing the other cues he may be responding to. Your aim is to limit as many signals as possible other than the actual command words that you speak. Try it, it's harder than it sounds.

**FADING YOUR PHYSICAL CUES**

**1** Choose a command that your dog knows very well, such as the "Sit" or "Down." Face your dog and ask him to perform this action as you normally would.

| | **INTERACTIVE GAME** |
|---|---|
| | Dog and Owner |
| **LOCATION** | In your hotel room or even outside if there are few distractions. |
| **LEVEL OF DIFFICULTY** | ☆☆☆ |
| | **Good brain workout** |
| **PROPS** | Treats |

**NO CHEATING!**

To be successful you will have to learn to remain still and to avoid giving any accidental responses that your dog may see and interpret.

When you have established a training method, perhaps incorporating hand signals to back up a verbal cue, it is remarkably hard to stand stock-still and poker-faced to play this game. Try it and see for yourself.

When you've got your back to your dog, you can't see what he is doing without turning round. Either use a mirror or ask a friend to let you know if he's doing it right.

**2** Ask him to do this again but this time you should keep your arms folded, or by your side, or behind your back. Gradually try to eliminate any gestures or movements that may be seen as signals by your dog.

**3** If he can succeed with this stage, you can then begin to turn your back on your dog and request the same action. If he performs as he is meant to, praise him well for getting it right.

**TIP** If your dog is confused or getting it wrong, stop and make things easier again. If he doesn't know the command word, then that's OK; you now know that you need to practice the game more and work on building associations with the cue word.

**EXTEND YOUR RANGE**
**1** Once you have achieved these basic commands, start to try others that you feel your dog understands well. After a "Sit" it is a natural follow-on to attempt a "Down."

**2** Challenge your dog to see how many he can do successfully without any further help from you.

# WATER GAMES

Dogs often enjoy water just as we do. They like to splash, swim and romp about in the shallows. Some breeds take to water naturally, but even those who are less keen can often be encouraged to play in it. This is easier with younger dogs, but if taken slowly, many can overcome their initial caution.

While it can be an enjoyable medium, water can also be extremely dangerous for dogs. They can drown or cut themselves on unseen sharp items under the surface. They may pick up water-borne infections or parasites, be made ill by pollution or even be bitten by poisonous or dangerous animals in certain locations.

Always think carefully before encouraging your dog into any body of water. Luckily, there are some fun water games that you can arrange at home, making them as safe as they can possibly be.

Be prepared for your dog to have a good shake after playing in water. Help him dry out by giving him a good rub with a towel afterwards to prevent him getting a chill.

# BOBBING FOR TREATS

A light basin could be easily overturned by an enthusiastic dog so choose one of an appropriate size and weight for your dog. Fill it about two-thirds full with water to weigh it down further while allowing enough space to prevent major spillage when your dog dips his feet or head into the basin. The lip of the basin makes it necessary for the dog to pick the floating item out of the water rather than pawing it to the side.

| | INTERACTIVE GAME |
|---|---|
| | Dog and Owner |
| **LOCATION** | Outside or in a room with a water-resistant floor. |
| **LEVEL OF DIFFICULTY** | ☆ ☆ **Moderate brain tester** <br> Teach "Take It" first. |
| **PROPS** | Basin with water and treats that float, dog towel and a mat for placing under the basin if playing indoors. |

Don't fill the basin right to the brim with water. Your dog is bound to displace some when he puts his face and paws in, and it will slop on the floor.

**DIPPING DOWN FOR TREATS**

**1** Float one of your dog's larger food treats on the water and encourage your dog to "Take it." If your dog is more motivated by toys, then float a favorite ball on the surface.

**2** Some more sensitive dogs can gradually build up a tolerance of putting their nose in the water if you help by scooping the treat in your hand and holding it on the surface of the water. Each time you do this you can lower your hand into the water a fraction further.

**3** Your dog may initially try to paw the water to get the treat or toy but will soon learn that he has to actually grab the item with his mouth to get it out of the basin. It is important to praise his early attempts, even if they fail, since otherwise he might give up.

**4** Eventually, your dog will be able to take the treat or toy straight from the surface. Practice with differently sized treats and toys for fun. You could even place different toys on the surface and ask him to pick out a specific item. (N.b. Teaching the Toy Identity Parade game first may help.)

This shallow basin is a convenient height for a small dog who can get his face and paws in the water without having to clamber over the lip.

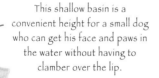

# DUNKING AND DIVING

When your dog is comfortable enough to put his nose into the water basin to pick up floating items, you can try to progress to this game which involves retrieving submerged treasure. Not all dogs are prepared to submerge their whole face but many can learn to play and enjoy this game. If your dog is worried by water, make sure you take this very slowly or even try other types of games instead.

**TAKING THE PLUNGE**
Some dogs adore water and will "dive" right in straight away. The majority of dogs, however, will need to be desensitized to the feeling of water being over their main sense organs: the nose, eyes and possibly even the ears. In that case it can help to start by getting your dog used to picking up a floating toy first.

**TIP** Unless it is a warm day, take care that your dog does not become too cold. This is especially important for dogs that were not bred to work around water and whose coats will offer little protection from the chill. Towel him dry afterwards.

| | INTERACTIVE GAME |
|---|---|
| | **Dog and Owner** |
| **LOCATION** | Outside or in a room with a water-resistant floor. |
| **LEVEL OF DIFFICULTY** | ☆☆☆ **Good brain workout** |
| **PROPS** | Child's wading pool or large basin, large jug with water, treats that sink, dog towel and a mat for placing under basin if playing indoors. |

# THE GREAT WATER RACE

Group races with your friends and their dogs are a great way to entertain yourselves and keep your dogs amused. If you have enough space, be imaginative and add in some other obstacles.

**BASIC RULES**
• Remember your training and never pull or jerk your dog even though you are rushing about.
• Dogs should be praised for good behavior and rewarded with a treat.

| | INTERACTIVE GAME |
|---|---|
| | **Several pairs of dogs/owners** |
| **LOCATION** | Outside with space for weaving poles or other obstacle items. |
| **LEVEL OF DIFFICULTY** | ☆☆☆ **Good brain workout** |
| **PROPS** | Basin of water, plastic cups, dogs on leads, large measuring jugs (one per person). |

**1** Choose a wading pool or a large basin, depending upon the size of your dog. Place your basin on the floor with just enough water in it to cover the bottom. Drop your sinkable treat into the water and then encourage your dog to "Take it."

**2** Very gradually pour a little more water into the basin and repeat the game so that your dog gets used to getting his nose wet a little at a time. Increase the water depth as your dog's confidence grows. Use very tasty treats to keep him interested.

**3** Keep the game enticing by teasing your dog with a toy before throwing it into the water. Your dog will have to dive in to retrieve his sunken treasure.

Owners should loop their dog's lead over one hand which will also be used to hold the cup.

**DASH FOR THE LINE**

The simplest way to play this game is to set up some cones or poles for each owner/dog team to weave carefully around, trying to keep the dog "walking nicely" as they go along. Of course, the more the dog pulls or jumps, the more water will be spilt.

Begin by placing your basin of water at the starting line. Each owner should take a plastic cup and hold a treat in their other hand if they want to lure their dog round the course. On the "Go" signal, each owner should scoop their cup in the water and start the race. Upon reaching the final line the owner should pour their remaining water into their waiting jug. If you are working as a relay team, the next pair should then start. If not, the winner is the pair who managed to transfer the most water from start to finish.

# GAMES FOR LESS ACTIVE DOGS

If you're reading this book and wondering which games your elderly or less mobile dog can play, then the answer really depends upon his fitness levels and body shape. Some older dogs can be incredibly fit and agile while others are visibly slow. Dogs that have physical problems that limit their mobility may also have difficulty with some of the more active games. However, there are many that they can attempt including those listed in this chapter. Of course, dogs that are physically fit can learn all of these too. Remember to use stronger tasting rewards and clear signals and commands for elderly dogs that have lost some of their sensory capacity.

**2** Advance this game by placing a treat on the other paw and repeat the lesson. Once he can do it on each paw individually, try placing a treat on both paws at the same time. Always remember to tell him to "Take it" when the time is right.

## BALANCE A TREAT ON YOUR PAW

This is a great game for dogs that have slowed down or who physically can't jump around any longer (though challenge yourself to teach your young boisterous dog too, if you have one).

| | INTERACTIVE GAME |
|---|---|
| | **Dog and Owner** |
| **LOCATION** | Any space where your dog can lie down comfortably. |
| **LEVEL OF DIFFICULTY** | ☆ ☆ **Moderate brain tester** Teach "Take it" and "Leave it" first. |
| **PROPS** | Treats — ideally large and flat. |

**START THE GAME BY BALANCING A TREAT**

**1** Ask your dog to lie down. Carefully place a treat on one of his front paws. Withdraw it if he tries to grab the food. Tell him to "Leave" as you place the treat on his foot. After a moment tell him to "Take it" and praise him. Since he has been told to "Leave," he may hesitate, in which case encourage him by picking the treat up and offering it to him. Then gradually build up the time he has to wait before you tell him to "Take it."

**3** The ultimate aim is to teach your dog to take the treats in the order you indicate — for example "Left and Right."

**TIP** It is important that your dog should respond correctly to the two commands: "Take it" and "Leave it." If necessary, see pages 66–67 for a recap.

**4** Place a treat on both your dog's paws. Focus your dog on the treat on his left paw by closely pointing to it while saying "Left take it."

Practice each side individually (using the command "Right take it" for the right paw), so he has a chance to learn the word for both sides. Make it easier by indicating which paw you mean during the early stages. If he then goes to take the other treat, tell him to "Leave." Practice until he responds correctly and seems to know his left from his right.

# BALANCE A TREAT ON YOUR NOSE

This is a fun game which involves no exertion by the dog, just urge control and focus on your commands. Your dog balances the treat on his nose until you tell him to "Take it."

| | INTERACTIVE GAME Dog and Owner |
|---|---|
| **LOCATION** | Any comfortable location. |
| **LEVEL OF DIFFICULTY** | ☆ ☆ ☆ **Good brain workout** Teach a steady "Sit" first. |
| **PROPS** | Treats (large, flat ones are easiest). |

**THE GREAT BALANCING ACT**

**1** Ask your dog to "Sit" facing you. You can sit or stand depending on your dog's size. Gently hold your dog's muzzle with one hand while placing the treat on his nose with the other. Depending on your dog's face shape, the best balancing place may be at any point along the muzzle. As soon as he allows the treat to touch his nose, pick it up and tell him to "Take it."

# SHY DOG

The aim of this game is to teach your dog to bring a paw up over his nose, as if he were shy and hiding his face. It looks cute and is yet another activity to add to your dog's repertoire.

| | INTERACTIVE GAME Dog and Owner |
|---|---|
| **LOCATION** | Anywhere your dog is relaxed. |
| **LEVEL OF DIFFICULTY** | ☆ ☆ **Moderate brain tester** |
| **PROPS** | Small Post-it notes (or large ones cut into strips) and treats. |

**SETTING UP A STICKY SITUATION**

**1** Begin with your dog in a sitting position in front of you. Gently press one of the Post-it notes to the top of his muzzle.

**2** Next time allow the treat to sit for a moment longer before you offer it to him. (At this stage you are still gently stabilizing the muzzle with one hand.) Begin to signal the pause with a raised index finger much like that used when telling your dog to "Wait" or "Stay." At first this hand will be positioned close to the nose.

**3** Very gradually increase the length of time for which the treat is balanced, while slightly moving back from your dog.
After each pause tell your dog to "Take it." Some will drop their muzzle while others will flick their head up to get the treat. Either way is fine. Keep practicing until you can balance the treat, step back away from your dog, before telling him to "Take it."

**2** Most dogs will bring up a paw to try to remove the sticker. When he does this, offer praise and a treat. (If he has removed the Post-it, don't worry as you can use another for the next practice run.)

**3** Repeat this part until your dog is using a more defined movement whereby the paw is coming right up and over the nose. At this point you can add in your cue word, "Shy." Practice until your dog has associated the cue word with the action.

Gradually reduce the size of the Post-it sticker so that eventually your dog no longer requires this trigger and can respond to your cue word alone. Ask him "Are you shy?" and hopefully he'll respond with his most bashful pose.

**TIP** Never use strong sticky tape that would pull on your dog's hair when removed. This will put him off wanting to learn this game.

# SEARCH GAMES

If you own a dog with a keen search drive, you may like to encourage him to play games that channel these instincts. The key is to go slowly so that he understands each stage of the game before you move on. Each dog will have his own search technique so observe him and make use of his abilities.

**FIND THE HIDDEN TOY**

**1** While your dog is watching, place a treat or a toy underneath one pot. Encourage your dog to approach it. He will probably sniff at the pot first. Try to wait for him to paw at the pot before you praise him and turn it over.

# FASTEST CANINE EYE

| | **INTERACTIVE GAME** Dog and Owner |
|---|---|
| **LOCATION** | In a low distraction area. |
| **LEVEL OF DIFFICULTY** | ☆ ☆ **Moderate brain tester** |
| **PROPS** | Treats and at least three plant pots. |

He will be well motivated by the prospect of something tasty.

**TREATS INSTEAD OF TOYS**

**1** You can play an entertaining variation of this game by using tempting treats instead of toys. Firstly show your dog the treat and allow him to smell it.

## Advanced Version

Instead of choosing between a few pots, hide the treat within a sealed food container. When you first introduce the container place the lid on top but don't seal it. Allow your dog to approach the container and nudge or paw at it. When he does, praise him, lift the lid and offer him the treat. Then practice with the sealed tub which makes it harder to detect the scent (though not impossible). Slowly add in extra tubs. They should all be sealed up but only one should contain the food. If they are transparent then hide the treat inside some paper wrapping. Add similar paper inside each tub. The tubs will look the same, but only one will contain the prize.

**2** Add a second empty pot and practice asking your dog to select the one hiding the treat. Encourage him to use his nose by varying the position of the pots. You can add in your cue word at this point. Some people will use "Find it"; others like to use a new command.

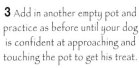

**3** Add in another empty pot and practice as before until your dog is confident at approaching and touching the pot to get his treat.

**4** If your dog picks the wrong pot, don't respond. He'll learn that he only gets a reward when he chooses the one covering the treat

**2** To begin with, you can let your dog see the pot in which you are concealing the treat, so he gets the idea of the game. Later you should keep the pot out of view as you hide the treat.

Despite the sealed lid, he has "nosed" out the right pot.

**4** When you are handling the tubs be careful not to touch the empty ones with hands that have been holding treats. If you smear any scent onto an empty tub, your dog may become confused when you tell him he has chosen the wrong one.

**3** If he selects the right one, praise him and then open the tub to let him have the treat (as above).

125

# OUT OF SIGHT BUT NOT OUT OF MIND

Once your dog can chase and retrieve toys that you throw, it is worth giving him an extra challenge. This is particularly of interest to working breeds with high search drives. Position yourself so that there is a barrier (for example, bushes or a hedge) between you and an open area where it's safe for your dog to run and fetch the toy. If you don't have a suitable barrier, create one by erecting a wind-break or a sheet hung between two chairs.

**RUSH ROUND THE BACK**

**1** Set yourself in front of the barrier having first made sure that there is nothing hazardous or likely to hurt your dog concealed behind it.

If you want to play this game in the safety of your garden, you can always create a barrier with a blanket and some supports.

**4** Encourage your dog to retrieve the toy to you. As you practice you can gradually throw the toy farther (you can move back from the barrier as well as throwing the toy a greater distance).

**5** Next, start to build up the time before you release your dog to go and find the toy you have thrown.

Dogs that enjoy a chase will love the energetic fetch and carry that this game requires.

| | INTERACTIVE GAME<br>Dog and Owner |
|---|---|
| **LOCATION** | In a safe outdoor area or in your garden. |
| **LEVEL OF DIFFICULTY** | ★★☆☆<br>**Advanced brain game**<br>Teach a reliable Retrieve first. |
| **PROPS** | A toy to retrieve and treats. |

**2** Position yourself a short distance (6–10ft/2–3m) from the barrier. Your dog can either be on a lead or in a "Sit stay" position. Show your dog the toy and then throw it so that it lands out of sight behind the barrier.

**3** Then release your dog and ask him to "Fetch it." Reward your dog for returning with the toy. Throw once or twice more before taking a short break.

He should rush behind the screen in pursuit.

You should have success if you use a toy that your dog is highly motivated to retrieve.

You want a nice, obedient release to keep the game going.

**6** Playing with two balls at once adds an extra challenge to this enjoyable and highly active game. It is also a great way of making sure your dog gets some beneficial exercise.

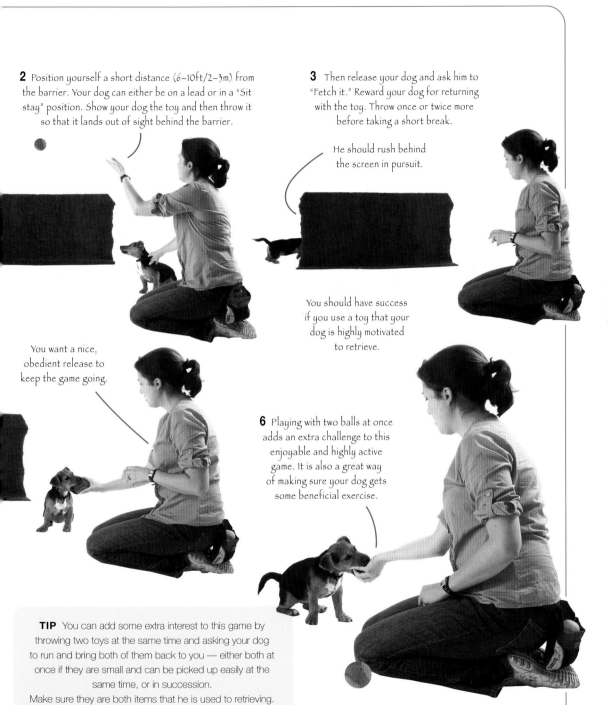

**TIP** You can add some extra interest to this game by throwing two toys at the same time and asking your dog to run and bring both of them back to you — either both at once if they are small and can be picked up easily at the same time, or in succession.
Make sure they are both items that he is used to retrieving.

# GO GET...

This is a game that is a challenge but it also has a very useful function. While everyone can benefit from playing this game, it is of particular relevance to owners who find it hard to move around or those who are deaf or hard of hearing and won't be able to hear their family's calls. The rest of us can use it when we are feeling lazy.

**PART 1**

**1** Decide who it would be most useful for your dog to "Go get." Once your dog has achieved good results in this game then you will be able to add in another person that your dog can "Go get." For this example, Ann will send the dog to get Claire.

**2** Ann should gently restrain her dog by his collar. Claire should tease him with a toy and then rush away to the opposite side of the room. Hopefully the dog will try to follow her. Ann should then say "Get Claire" and release the dog. He should be praised and well rewarded for running to Claire.

The dog should be released when Claire has rushed some distance away.

**3** Keep practicing over many sessions. Claire should move a little further away, then into another room. Claire should encourage the dog to rush and find her by squeaking or honking a dog toy. She should also encourage him with her voice. Always offer rewards for success. With practice, Ann will be able to send her dog all over the house to find Claire.

| | |
|---|---|
| | **INTERACTIVE GAME**<br>Dog and two people |
| **LOCATION** | In and around your home. |
| **LEVEL OF DIFFICULTY** | ☆ ☆ ☆ ☆<br>**Advanced brain game**<br>Teach a reliable Retrieve first. |
| **PROPS** | Teach a good recall and your choice of touch alert. |

Before continuing the game, Claire should practice asking her dog to "paw touch" her a few times. High value treats will ensure the dog is keen to perform the "touch" during the excitement of the "Go Get" game.

The game should be taken back a step to make it a little easier so that the extra task won't seem too much for the dog. Now, when he finds Claire he should be encouraged to "paw touch" her before praise and rewards are offered.

Practice will be necessary over several sessions.

**PART 2**

When Claire is found, it is helpful if the dog gets her attention so that she knows she's wanted. Otherwise there is a risk that she'll ignore the dog and miss the message.

The attention-getting action can take many forms. What you choose will depend upon your dog and your personal preferences. You may choose a nose nudge, a paw touch, jumping up or any other action that your dog can easily perform. A paw touch is commonly used.

Job done! Time for a treat...

**PART 3**

The final part to this great game is for Ann to encourage her dog to return back to her with Claire. Again, it is advisable to take the game back to a simpler level until this element has been added in successfully.

Ann should wait until her dog has given his alert signal to Claire. She should then call him or squeak his toy so that he returns. She should encourage him with an excited voice. Claire should return to Ann with him and then reward the dog.

With enough practice your dog should be able to run to "get" the person you want and then return to you for his reward. Apply these rules to whoever will be working with your dog.

**TIP** At this stage the game can be used to send messages to one another — perhaps if you're both working in different parts of the home. Tuck a note into your dog's collar before sending him off to find the other person.

129

# ARMCHAIR GAMES

While many games require both dog and owner to be very active, there are plenty of brain games that are suitable for less agile owners or for those who are poorly or perhaps just feeling exhausted after trying all the other energetic games in this book! Remember that mental stimulation is as important as physical exercise, so spend time encouraging your dog to learn some of these new tasks. You may find some of them useful too.

# REACH OUT AND TOUCH

If you like the technique of targeting your dog to touch a particular item (as discussed in Chapter 5), then you can use this to teach some Armchair Games. This will involve a target stick which is essentially a spherical marker mounted on the end of a stick. These can be purchased or home-made. They act as an extension of your arm which makes many maneuvers easier. It is possible to just use your hand but you won't be able to reach out as far and you will have to bend down lower too.

# HOW DO YOU DO ?

Encouraging your dog to bow should be fairly easy since all dogs will adopt this position when they want to play and will even do so when they are stretching forward to lengthen their spines.

| | INTERACTIVE GAME |
|---|---|
| | **Dog and Owner** |
| **LOCATION** | Anywhere your dog is comfortable. |
| **LEVEL OF DIFFICULTY** | ☆ ☆ **Moderate brain tester** |
| **PROPS** | Treats and a target stick. |

**BOW DOWN PLEASE**
**1** Begin with your dog standing nearby. Spend a little time getting him used to touching the target stick with his nose.

**2** Once your dog is readily touching the end of the stick wherever you hold it, you can use it to teach different games without having to be so active yourself.

**FIRST TEACH THE NOSE TOUCH**

**1** Teach your dog to "nose touch" your target stick as described in Chapter 5. You should reward your dog every time he touches the end of the stick with his nose. Get your timing right or you might find you accidentally reward him for biting or licking the stick, which will slow down your progress.

You want your dog to target the end of the stick at whatever height it is held.

Target sticks are normally telescopic so that you can adjust the length.

**TIP** Be quick to reward as if you wait too long he will probably sink into a full Down position.

**2** Then slowly move it downwards from his nose towards the area between his paws. In order to touch the marker it is most comfortable for your dog to bow down. As soon as he does, praise him and reward him.

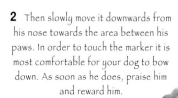

**TIP** You can also use your target stick to help you teach your dog to spin and to dance (Chapter 15).

The action of following the target stick down should lead to a bow.

# HOP OVER

If your dog is mature and physically fit, you could teach him to jump even if you can't get up and move around with him. This is much easier with small to medium dogs as they can maneuver themselves in a smaller space.

A treat held in your hand is an effective lure.

| | **INTERACTIVE GAME**<br>Dog and Owner |
|---|---|
| **LOCATION** | Where your dog is relaxed and comfortable but with space to take off and land. |
| **LEVEL OF DIFFICULTY** | ☆ ☆ Moderate brain tester |
| **PROPS** | A walking stick and treats. A foot rest may be useful. |

**HOP OVER A LEG**

**1** To get your dog used to the game, you can start by simply luring him to walk over your outstretched leg.

Use the same methods as described in Jump Over (see Chapter 4) using a stick or your legs stretched out in front of you. These will form the first level of your jump. Keep practicing until he can jump over your feet on cue. The easiest way to do this is to rest your feet or the end of your stick on a foot stool. This game is an easy way to encourage your dog to be active even on those days when you can't get up and about.

Keep the jump low when you are playing with a small dog.

**2** As he learns the action and gains in confidence, encourage him to speed up and actually make a little jump to clear the leg.

### HOP OVER A STICK

**1** If you get tired of keeping your leg stretched out in front of you, you can use a walking stick or sturdy cane instead. This also has the advantage that you avoid the risks of bumps and bruises if the dog misjudges the jump. As with all jumping games, make sure that the take-off and landing areas are clear and not slippery.

**2** Try to get your dog to jump equally confidently in both directions back and forth across the stick. In this way you avoid favoring one side over the other. You can also slowly raise the height of the jump. But be realistic about what is reasonable.

### RAISING THE BAR

Once your dog is proving proficient at jumping over your leg as your foot rests on the floor, it is time to up the ante! Find a footstool or upturned waterpaper basket and rest your foot on that. Now you have quite a challenging hurdle for your dog to tackle.

The end of the stick can be slowly lifted off the floor towards the horizontal.

**TIP** If you have a very large dog, it is not advisable to use your legs as jumps in case he accidentally lands on you. Use a stick, a garden cane or an umbrella instead.

# SNEEZE AND RETRIEVE!

Start by making sure your dog is happy to pick up and retrieve a handkerchief or tissue.

Many dogs love this game as this is the only time they are allowed to touch tissues! Practice asking your dog to fetch a tissue placed on the floor. It can really help in the later stages of this game if you gesture towards the tissue with your hand when you send him to "Fetch it."

The aim of this game is to teach your dog to fetch a tissue when he hears the cue "Atchoo" sound.

Start with a tissue resting on the box.

| INTERACTIVE GAME | |
|---|---|
| **Dog and Owner** | |
| **LOCATION** | In your home. |
| **LEVEL OF DIFFICULTY** | ☆☆☆☆ |
| | **Advanced brain game** Teach a good "Retrieve" first. |
| **PROPS** | A box of tissues or a handkerchief and treats. |

**TIME FOR A TISSUE**

**1** Once he can retrieve a tissue from the floor, place one on top of a tissue box and practice a retrieve from this new position. When he has learned only to grab a tissue when he hears the cue "Fetch it," you can begin to use an open box of tissues. (Until then, put them away between sessions or you may end up with tissues strewn everywhere.)

# SAY YOUR PRAYERS

This is a cute trick that most dogs can learn to do if you are patient. Encourage your dog to come up close and sit next to you. Hold a treat to his nose and move it slowly upwards so that he has to stretch up to follow it. As he rises onto his haunches, his paws should lift up and come to rest on your arm, leg or chair.

| INTERACTIVE GAME | |
|---|---|
| **Dog and Owner** | |
| **LOCATION** | Any room where your dog is comfortable. |
| **LEVEL OF DIFFICULTY** | ☆☆☆☆ |
| | **Advanced brain game** It's easier if your dog can already sit back on his haunches. |
| **PROPS** | Treats and a target stick. |

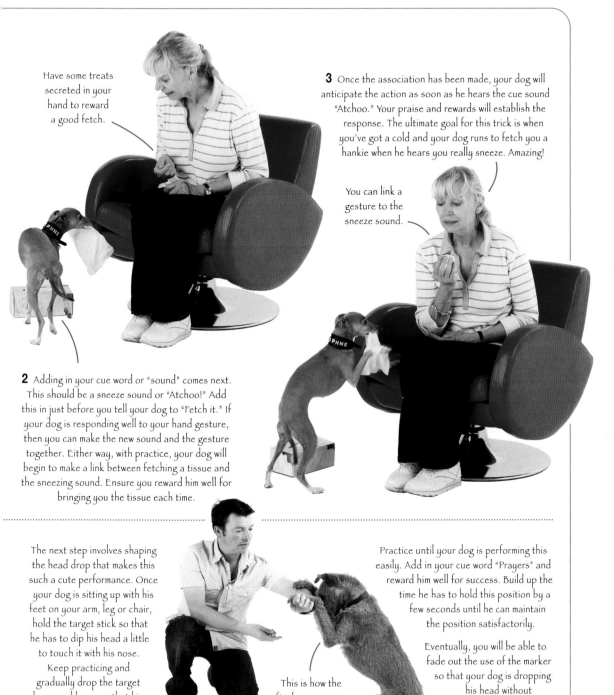

Have some treats secreted in your hand to reward a good fetch.

**3** Once the association has been made, your dog will anticipate the action as soon as he hears the cue sound "Atchoo." Your praise and rewards will establish the response. The ultimate goal for this trick is when you've got a cold and your dog runs to fetch you a hankie when he hears you really sneeze. Amazing!

You can link a gesture to the sneeze sound.

**2** Adding in your cue word or "sound" comes next. This should be a sneeze sound or "Atchoo!" Add this in just before you tell your dog to "Fetch it." If your dog is responding well to your hand gesture, then you can make the new sound and the gesture together. Either way, with practice, your dog will begin to make a link between fetching a tissue and the sneezing sound. Ensure you reward him well for bringing you the tissue each time.

The next step involves shaping the head drop that makes this such a cute performance. Once your dog is sitting up with his feet on your arm, leg or chair, hold the target stick so that he has to dip his head a little to touch it with his nose. Keep practicing and gradually drop the target lower and lower so that his head moves into the desired position.

This is how the final prayer pose should look.

Practice until your dog is performing this easily. Add in your cue word "Prayers" and reward him well for success. Build up the time he has to hold this position by a few seconds until he can maintain the position satisfactorily.

Eventually, you will be able to fade out the use of the marker so that your dog is dropping his head without needing it.

# FETCH THE BOWL

This is an extension of a "Find it" command where your dog searches for an item by name. Of course, your dog will always know where his bowl is kept so there is less chance of confusion here. In addition, your dog will already have developed good associations with the bowl since he is fed from it every day.

| | |
|---|---|
| | **INTERACTIVE GAME**<br>Dog and Owner |
| **LOCATION** | Any room where your dog is comfortable. |
| **LEVEL OF DIFFICULTY** | ☆ ☆ ☆<br>**Good brain workout**<br>This is easier if your dog can already Retrieve and Carry it. |
| **PROPS** | Dog bowl and treats. |

Firstly you will have to make sure that your dog can pick up the bowl. Many bowls have curved sides or are shaped in such a way that can be very difficult for a dog to lift. However, with practice most dogs become confident and manage to do this. If the bowl is too difficult, then begin with an easier, lighter version.

**TIP** It is not a good idea to ask your dog to lift up a ceramic bowl since this could easily break if he were to drop it on a hard floor.

**TAKE A BOWL FROM THE HAND**

**1** Begin by getting your dog's attention. Offer him the bowl and encourage him to "Take it" from you. When he does take it into his mouth, praise him and give him a reward. Initially let him hold it for just a few seconds.

This plastic bowl has a nice shape that makes it easy for the dog to carry.

**2** Gradually increase the time that you ask him to hold the bowl before you offer him the reward. When he can comfortably hold the bowl, begin to encourage him to carry it to you.

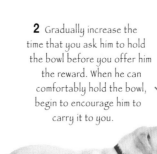

**PICK UP FROM THE FLOOR**

**1** Now that your dog knows how to hold, carry and retrieve the bowl, he is ready to learn to pick it up by himself.

**2** Put the bowl on the floor and encourage your dog to pick it up by telling him to "Take it." As soon as he does, praise and reward him. Practice this until you are sure that he is happy to pick up the bowl when you ask him to do so.

**PICK UP AND CARRY**

Once he can perform each part of this game it is time to join them up. Ask him to pick up the bowl and then encourage him to carry it to you. Add in your verbal cue now that the action is complete. You could choose a cue such as "Bowl" but it may be more fun to use the term "Hungry." Introduce the new cue immediately prior to saying the old cue "Take it." Once he has made the link with the new cue word, you can drop out the old one.

**3** Offer him the bowl and then take a few steps back. Encourage him to "Fetch" the bowl to you and reward him for doing so. Repeat your training until your dog can confidently bring the bowl to you from a place that is closer and closer to the place where it normally sits.

# CHANGING CHANNELS

We have all been in that situation when we have just got comfy in our chair and then realize that the TV remote control is across the room. So why not give your dog a job to do by teaching him to fetch the remote for you?

| | INTERACTIVE GAME |
|---|---|
| | **Dog and Owner** |
| **LOCATION** | Usually in the living area of your home where you watch TV. |
| **LEVEL OF DIFFICULTY** | ☆☆☆ **Good brain workout** Teach a "Find it" and a "Retrieve" first. |
| **PROPS** | An old TV remote control with bateries removed and treats. Eventually a real remote. |

### ADDING THE CUE WORD

**1** Add in your cue word "Remote" by saying it prior to the original "Find it" cue. Once you have repeated it often enough, your dog will begin to anticipate the game when he hears the new cue word.

**2** Once the association has been made you can drop out the old "Find it" cue completely.

### TAKE THE REMOTE

**1** Begin by asking your dog to "Take" the remote from you. Praise and reward him for taking hold of it.

**2** Once your dog is taking the remote happily, begin to play a "Find it" game with him. Allow your dog to see you placing it in different places and then release him to go and "Find it" and pick it up.

**3** Ensure that you reward him well for finding it successfully. Keep practicing until you are confident that your dog can find and bring you the remote control each time you ask him to.

Make sure he delivers it to your hand.

### SAFETY ADVICE

It is important to begin training with an old remote control that contains no batteries. This is because your dog may become over-excited at first and you have to ensure that he is going to be sufficiently safe to play this game "for real." When your dog has learned that he should only bring you the remote when asked for it and you are sure he will not play with it, then you can exchange it for the genuine remote control.

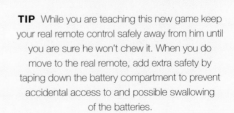

**TIP** While you are teaching this new game keep your real remote control safely away from him until you are sure he won't chew it. When you do move to the real remote, add extra safety by taping down the battery compartment to prevent accidental access to and possible swallowing of the batteries.

# GAMES FOR SPECIFIC BREEDS

## TERRIERS

Most terriers still have their ancestors' instincts to "go to ground." The word terrier actually derives from the Latin word *terra* which means earth, so these are literally "earth dogs." Although people keep terriers predominantly as pets nowadays, they are still known for their high activity levels, outgoing and sometimes feisty natures and tenacious characters.

If you own a terrier you will probably be aware of these traits and know that you must be extra wary while on country walks, since your little dog may dart down an animal hole without warning. However, there are safe ways for your dog to satisfy his natural urges without either risking an emergency situation or harming any small animal.

If you have some space in your garden you can create your own system of tunnels which can be as simple or as complicated as you like. Wide piping can be purchased from your local builder or plumbing equipment stores. You may also be able to find recycled sections because you won't necessarily require much. The pipe should be wide enough for your dog to easily fit through. Do not risk using pipe of too small a diameter as it is important that your dog can get through without any danger of becoming stuck.

Many people can encourage their dog to have fun just by placing the pipes on the ground and encouraging the dog through as described in the Tunnel Dash game. However, owners who want a more intensive terrier game can spend time creating partially sunken tunnels.

If you are going to sink pipes into the ground, you do need to consider your location. If your garden is below the water table, you risk flooding. If you live in an area where poisonous snakes reside, or where other dangerous animals may take shelter in the tunnel, you should take precautions by fitting stoppers on the ends of the pipe-work after each game.

Tie a long line to a small furry toy.

Run this line through the pipe, leaving the end with the toy exposed at the entrance. The line should run through the tunnel and out of the exit so that you have plenty of length with which to hold and pull it through.

When your dog approaches the pipe, haul on the line to pull the toy down into the tunnel as fast as you can. Keep pulling so your dog has to charge through the pipe and out the other side to catch the toy. You might find that attaching the toy to a reel can make reeling the toy in much easier and faster.

If your dog loves this game you should consider joining an earth-dog group where they have much more interesting tunnel set-ups and where the element of competition makes it more exciting for everyone (see Chapter 16).

**DOWN THE TUBE**
Little terriers usually love the idea of squeezing down narrow tunnels in search of prey. You can harness this instinct by playing chase games that encourage your dog to dash through a length of piping.

Use a pipe wide enough to allow your dog run through.

# SCENTHOUNDS

Scenthounds have an incredible ability to detect minute levels of scent. Their nasal passageways are especially densely provided with scent receptors. Scenthound bodies are also adapted to maximize their ability to detect scent. They tend to have longer ears and loose facial skin to help direct the flow of scent towards the dog's nose. Many owners of scenthounds have to work very hard to keep their dog responsive to them on walks as they can easily become focused on a scent trail that their owner is oblivious to, and dash off to follow it.

Then you can move over more varieties of terrain including through long grass and over tarmac for added interest.

Create a trail using highly scented foods, such as meat scraps, fish or cheese, stuffed into the foot of an old pair of tights. Either walk the trail yourself before taking your dog out or ask a friend to walk a few minutes ahead of you, trailing the tights along the ground as they go.

Clip your dog's lead on, ideally using a harness to limit any pulling on his neck as he follows the scent. If your dog always walks nicely on a lead and collar, use a harness just for scent games so that he is free to pull and so that your heelwork training doesn't suffer.

When your dog is actively following the trail you can urge him to "Track." Praise and encourage him as you go along making sure that he discovers a wonderfully tasty reward at the end of the trail to keep him keen.

### FOLLOW YOUR NOSE

Scenthounds like Bassets have remarkably sensitive senses of smell. Their large, drooping ears help to channel scents towards their noses.

A scenthound on the trail will pull strongly. Use a harness to distribute the load more evenly.

Lay the trail a short while before you plan to go tracking.

Create your own scent trails to stimulate your dog. Each dog will have a slightly different way of following a scent. As amateur detectives you and your dog should be able to follow a highly scented trail successfully.

You may want to begin in your own garden or in an outdoor area where there will be little other distraction. Begin with very simple trails until your dog catches on to the game.

**TIP** The extraordinary sensitivity that scenthounds have to odors does have a disadvantage — it can be difficult to keep their attention when training if they are distracted by a scent in the air. It helps to use highly flavored/scented food treats to maintain focus.

# HERDING DOGS

Not many owners of herding dogs also own a herd of sheep to practice with. Luckily there are many places where young herding dogs can be taken to train with experienced dogs and dog-savvy sheep. For the rest of us, there are games we can play at home that can take advantage of our herding breed's instincts as well as instilling extra control over their movements at a distance from us.

**ONE WOMAN AND HER DOG**
If you watch herding dogs, you will start to see that they tend to run in a wide arc rather than a straight line. Training these dogs takes advantage of this by teaching them to run in either a clockwise direction ("Come by") or an anti-clockwise direction ("Away to me"). These movements can be combined with a stop signal ("Stand" or "Down") and a slow approach ("Walk up") to provide the basic instruction your dog would need to know for herding work.

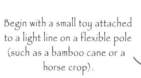

Begin with a small toy attached to a light line on a flexible pole (such as a bamboo cane or a horse crop).

# SIGHTHOUNDS

Sighthounds' speed and love of chasing is well known. They will often chase a toy that is thrown but when it stops moving they often grow disinterested in the game, leaving you to retrieve the toy yourself. You can take advantage of your dog's natural instincts to chase a small item that is moving along the ground, while remaining in control of the game.

**THE FUN OF THE CHASE**
**1** Attach a soft toy to the end of a light long line. A riding crop linked to the line and toy works well since it allows you to flick the toy and move it quickly along the ground.

Begin by moving the toy to your right in a clockwise direction. As your dog moves in this direction give your command "Come by." Praise him for following the toy.

When you change direction and encourage him to run to the left, or anti-clockwise, you can introduce your command, "Away to me."

Begin with slower movements at first so that you have complete control and so that your dog doesn't become so excited that he tries to leap and grab at the toy.

Many collie-type dogs will stop when the animal they are "herding" stops. When your dog is following the toy, stop moving it and add in the appropriate cue word "Down" or "Stand" when your dog pauses.

Teach your dog to move directly towards the toy by slowly dragging it along the ground towards you. As he creeps forward add the cue "Walk Up."

Practice all of these commands separately during many training sessions until you have good control over your dog's movements around you.

**ABOVE** You can learn many more commands and training techniques for controlling flocks of sheep by joining a herding group that specializes in this particular activity.

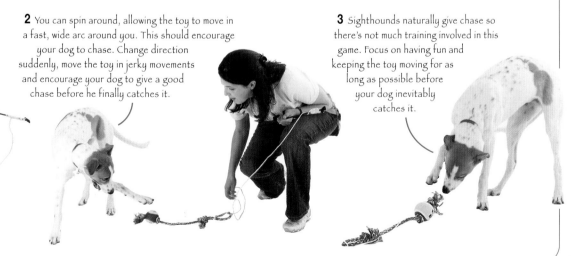

**2** You can spin around, allowing the toy to move in a fast, wide arc around you. This should encourage your dog to chase. Change direction suddenly, move the toy in jerky movements and encourage your dog to give a good chase before he finally catches it.

**3** Sighthounds naturally give chase so there's not much training involved in this game. Focus on having fun and keeping the toy moving for as long as possible before your dog inevitably catches it.

# PARTY GAMES

Everyone likes to have mastered a good joke or a trick that they can perform for family or friends. If you have a clever dog to hand, your guests are bound to be even more impressed. Also, seeing the same dog trick more than once is fine; telling the same joke rarely is! While lots of the brain games are entertaining and great to watch, here are some more ideas to try.

**START WITH ONE PAW**

**1** Many dogs will offer a paw naturally. You can then add a hand signal and cue word very easily. For all other dogs you will have to teach them to offer their foot.

## SHAKE A PAW

This is a common choice in most dog owner's trick repertoire. Teaching your dog to give you paws on command makes drying feet, cutting nails and checking pads much easier.

**PROGRESS TO AN OPEN HAND**

Once your dog has really got the hang of Shake A Paw, you should be able to dispense with the treat concealed in your hand. Your verbal cue and proffered open palm should be enough to get the right response.

| | **INTERACTIVE GAME** Dog and Owner |
|---|---|
| **LOCATION** | Begin in a quiet, comfortable area. |
| **LEVEL OF DIFFICULTY** | ☆ Easy brain exercise |
| **PROPS** | Treats. |

**RIGHT AND LEFT**

**1** Once your dog has become proficient at offering both paws on request, you can build a fun trick out of it. Ask him to give you a right...

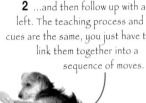

**2** ...and then follow up with a left. The teaching process and cues are the same, you just have to link them together into a sequence of moves.

**2** Start by sitting in front of your dog with your treat in your closed hand. Reach the hand with the treat in it out to your dog and hold it in front of him at his chest height and allow him to sniff at it. Dogs with long backs or arthritis won't be able to lift their paws very high so adjust by holding your hand lower down.

**3** Hold the hand still while he sniffs. Most dogs will eventually try to paw at your hand to get at the treat. As soon as he lifts his paw up, open your hand to release the reward. Some dogs will begin by only lifting their paw slightly off the floor. Reward this anyway with a treat as you can easily shape the action into a bigger lift with practice.

**TIP** Most dogs will try to paw you for attention or rewards. Make sure you only respond when you've asked for the action otherwise you risk encouraging the habit.

**NOW THE OTHER ONE...**
Once you have successfully taught your dog to Shake A Paw on command, you can teach him to lift the other paw. To encourage this you should hold your treat hand closer to the opposite leg or even use your other hand. You should use a different verbal cue, such as "Other one." Be patient and don't respond when he lifts the original foot.

**4** Once your dog is confidently placing his paw in your hand, you can start to say your verbal command "Shake paw." Practice until he can offer you the paw quickly on hearing the command.

Remember to give a treat from the other hand once your dog has lifted his paw and placed it in your hand.

The right hand attracts the dog to raise a left paw.

# WAVING HI AND GOODBYE

To encourage the "wave" motion you should try the Shake A Paw game as normal but hold your hand a little further away from him so he has to reach out in an attempt to touch it. As his paw reaches out, praise him and give the reward. Repeat this stage as often as necessary until your dog is doing the action easily.

| | INTERACTIVE GAME Dog and Owner |
|---|---|
| **LOCATION** | Anywhere. Looks great at your door when greeting or seeing off guests. |
| **LEVEL OF DIFFICULTY** | ☆ ☆ **Moderate brain tester** Teach "Sit" and "Shake A Paw" first. |
| **PROPS** | Treats. |

**HOW TO START TEACHING A WAVE**

**1** To teach this game you want your dog to reach up with his paw but actually to miss touching your hand. The result is that he will appear to be waving his paw in the air.

**SIT UP AND WAVE**

**1** If your dog is physically healthy enough to sit back on his haunches then he can be taught to sit up and wave his paws together. Dogs are often a little unsteady when they first try this so don't rush him. Ask your dog to sit. Hold a treat close to his nose, allowing him to sniff it.

**2** Slowly move the treat so that it moves upwards and above your dog's head. To follow it your dog will have to sit up and back onto his haunches. Release the reward the moment he does this. Over the next few sessions you will teach him to rise up and hold the position for longer.

**3** The next step is to add in your "Wave" command which your dog already knows. You may have to go back to getting him to touch your hand with his paw but he should be able to quickly move on to the familiar "Wave." Keep rewarding good attempts until he is waving reliably.

**2** When your dog is in a Sit, extend your hand holding the treat in front of him, but have it a little higher that you did for Shake A Paw.

**TIP** Some dogs show little interest when offered a hand containing a treat. If your dog is like this, you may need to spur him on with a specially excited tone of voice.

**3** Just as he gives his waving motion, you can start to move your own hand in a little wave. You can also add in your verbal command "Wave."

**STANDING WAVE**

If your dog has a long back or problems sitting up on his haunches, then he can learn to wave while standing. The same techniques are used to encourage your dog to reach out to your hand. Repeat this until he is confidently pawing the air. Introduce your verbal cue and you have a "waving" dog!

**4** Give a treat and words of praise as soon as you get the correct reaction. Practice until he can offer you the action as soon as he sees or hears your signal.

A tasty tidbit is a great motivator.

# SPINNING AROUND AND AROUND

Spinning around is a game that can be slow and steady, or fast and exciting depending upon your dog's physical size and fitness.

| | INTERACTIVE GAME |
|---|---|
| | **Dog and Owner** |
| **LOCATION** | In an area where your dog can turn around safely. |
| **LEVEL OF DIFFICULTY** | ☆ Easy brain exercise |
| **PROPS** | Treats or a toy. |

**TIP** Dogs can display compulsive spinning behavior which may lead to physical problems. If this applies to your dog, then try to teach an alternative game instead. On the other hand, teaching an attention-seeking spinner to twirl on cue is useful since the dog learns that it's only worth doing this when he is asked to (as rewards only arrive then).

**CLOCKWISE SPINS**

**1** Hold a treat and allow your dog to sniff it. Slowly move the treat around to one side of your dog so he has to turn his head to maintain contact with it. Initially you should reward this small movement, even though it's only about a quarter of a spin.

**NOW ANTI-CLOCKWISE**

**1** It is good to teach your dog to spin equally confidently in both directions. Use the same luring technique but the other way round.

**2** Add in your cue word. Choose one word for a clockwise turn and a different one for anti-clockwise. Example cues could be: "Twist" and "Spin."

Most dogs will prefer spinning one way to the other, so aim to master that first.

**2** Bit by bit you can lure your dog around in a circle, rewarding improvement as you go.

**REDUCING HAND MOVEMENT**
Once your dog has associated the cue with the turning action, you can begin to minimize your hand gesture. Make the circle higher and smaller as you practice.

**3** Gradually lure your dog further around until he can happily turn 360 degrees in pursuit of your hand. Reward him well each time he follows the lure around.

Initially keep your hand moving in quite a low circle above the dog's head.

Eventually you should just give a small flick of the hand, as if you were starting to make the "circle" lure. He should happily twirl around if he's understood the game.

**3** It is better to teach each direction at different times to prevent confusion. Remember which cue is linked to which direction!

**4** Some dogs are reluctant to go all the way round in the early stages of learning. Make sure that you reward even a small move in the right direction; next time you may get a little bit more.

# ROLLIN' ROVER

The roll-over can follow on nicely from the "Down" action and is suitable for dogs of any age as long as they are healthy. Very large breeds may find it harder to heave themselves over so you should make the judgement about your dog's physical ability.

**TEACHING A ROLL**
**1** Begin with your dog in a Down position in front of you.

|  | **INTERACTIVE GAME**<br>**Dog and Owner** |
|---|---|
| **LOCATION** | On any floor surface where your dog is comfortable lying down. |
| **LEVEL OF DIFFICULTY** | ☆ ☆ **Moderate brain tester** |
| **PROPS** | Treats. |

Decide which way you want your dog to roll. This can depend on how he tends to lie on his hips. If his hips are turned to one particular side, it is easier to opt to roll from that side over.

**INTRODUCE A COMMAND**
**1** Once he has got the knack of rolling over easily by following the lure, you can introduce the command word just as he goes over — "Roll."

**ROLL OVER AND OVER AND OVER**
With enough practice your dog will be able to repeat the roll several times in a row for extra effect. At first you may have to reward each roll, but once your dog is eager, he may do a series for one bumper reward at the end.

**3** Repeat this stage until your dog is very comfortable shifting over onto his side. The next stage is to continue the lure further so that he rolls his whole body onto his back. Reward your dog at this stage.

**2** Hold your treat to his nose and allow him to sniff. Slowly move your hand round to his shoulder so that he turns his head to follow it. If you go slowly enough, he should naturally shift his weight onto his shoulder. Release the treat once this stage is achieved.

Some dogs roll directly over from this position while others need you to continue the lure until they have completely rolled over. Break the movement down into as many parts as your dog requires.

**TIP** Watch your arm position when you are teaching the Roll; it should be bent in a wide arc around your dog to allow for his legs to roll around without hitting your arm.

**2** Repeat this every time he is about to do the roll and he will make the association between the verbal cue and the action you want him to perform. Eventually you will be able to say the command word and he'll be merrily rolling over.

**3** It always helps to offer a treat. The hand movement for this command is an arc due to the way you lure your dog over. At first this needs to be a large gesture but with practice you will be able to reduce this to just a small hand movement.

# PLAYING DEAD

Go for a touch of drama with your dog with the Playing Dead game. This one is great for entertaining your family and friends. This is a great option for dogs that are unable to perform the Rollin' Rover.

| | **INTERACTIVE GAME** | |
|---|---|---|
| | **Dog and Owner** | |
| **LOCATION** | On a floor where your dog can comfortably lie down. | |
| **LEVEL OF DIFFICULTY** | ★★★★☆ | |
| | **Advanced brain game** | |
| **PROPS** | Treats and a mat if the floor is cold or uncomfortable. | |

**FIRST TEACH YOUR DOG TO LIE ON HIS SIDE**

Begin with your dog in a Down position. Kneel in front of him and use a treat lure to slowly turn his head to one side. As it moves round, he should begin to lean on his shoulder and then move onto his side. Reward this movement but be prepared to accept smaller increments if your dog is not totally relaxed. Keep practicing until it is easy to get your dog onto his side. If he is not already doing so, lure his head so that he is lying completely flat on the floor. Then, begin to offer extra rewards so that he learns to lie there for longer.

# CRAWLING CANINE

The crawling action can be used by itself or as part of other games, such as Limbo Dancing, or chained together with other actions for a unique sequence of your own. Your dog's style of crawling will depend largely on his body shape and size. Smaller dogs tend to scuttle along while larger dogs often "bunny hop" along propelled by their back legs.

**FIRST USE A LURE**

**1** Begin with your dog in a Down position. Take a treat and allow your dog to sniff it. Very slowly draw the treat away from your dog so that in order to keep sniffing and licking at it, he has to shuffle forwards.

**THEN TEACH A SIGNAL**

**1** Once he is crawling forwards add in your cue word "Crawl" and keep praising him. With practice, your dog should be able to "crawl" farther.

| | **INTERACTIVE GAME** | |
|---|---|---|
| | **Dog and Owner** | |
| **LOCATION** | On any floor comfortable to lie on. | |
| **LEVEL OF DIFFICULTY** | ★☆ **Moderate brain tester** | |
| **PROPS** | Treats. | |

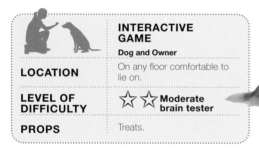

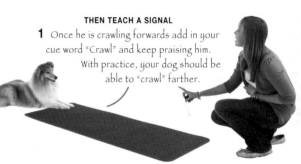

## NOW INTRODUCE A HAND SIGNAL

As you practice, you can begin to develop your hand signal for this game. The shape of your hand can change to create a "pistol" shape to add detail to the game. Eventually you will just make the "pistol" shape for your cue. Exaggerate the arc you make with your hand as you initially lure him over. This movement should be reduced very slowly. Your verbal cue for this party piece can be "Bang bang." Introduce this once your dog is going into position easily. If you don't like the idea of a play dead game, then just call it Faint or Lie Flat instead.

## TRY DIFFERENT POSITIONS

Practice until your dog can lie relaxed on the floor until you release him. Wait until he is lying still before praising and offering the treats. A wagging tail is a good indicator that he is having fun but it might spoil your performance! If you practice enough, he will be able to keel over from sitting or standing positions.

Add a final touch to the game by teaching him cover his eyes with his paw as he performs his dramatic Playing Dead role.

Bigger dogs often tend to lift their rear quarters.

**2** As soon as he does this, release the treat. Take this slowly and make sure you reward each forwards movement. If he gets up, just put him back into a Down and start again, taking it more slowly the next time.

**3** If he persistently gets up, try luring him under your leg or a chair so that you can reinforce the correct position.

**2** You will be able to stop holding treats and also use a more simple hand gesture to cue the action.

**TIP** If you have already taught your dog to touch a marker with his paws you can use this to encourage him to shuffle forwards. Hold the marker an inch ahead of your dog's paws. Reward him for shuffling forwards to touch it. Very slowly slide the marker away from him so he has to crawl to touch it again.

# BEDTIME !

This game looks great and always impresses friends and family. Your dog will lie on his blanket and when you say "Bedtime" he'll take hold of it and pull it over himself as if he is going to bed.

    This trick is made up from fairly simple movements but it can be difficult for dogs to chain all the parts together unless you break it down into small parts which should each be practiced thoroughly.

**START WITH YOUR DOG LEARNING TO LIE FLAT**

**1** Your dog should lie on one side of his blanket. Spend time teaching him to lie down flat, as in the Play Dead game. He should lie with his legs facing the center of the blanket.

He needs to feel very comfortable doing this before you move onto the next part of the party trick.

| | |
|---|---|
|  | **INTERACTIVE GAME**<br>**Dog and Owner** |
| **LOCATION** | Any location where your dog is relaxed and with space for him to lie down flat. |
| **LEVEL OF DIFFICULTY** | ☆☆☆☆☆<br>**A proper brainteaser**<br>First teach "Down," "Take it" and how to lie flat as in the Play Dead game. |
| **PROPS** | A blanket and treats. |

# MULTIPLE DOG PARTY TRICKS

If you own more than one dog then you can create games that involve them all. If you want to include party tricks, then you should focus on teaching each dog the action individually to begin with.

Then bring the dogs together. Some tricks look really great with multiple dogs. These include:

**DOUBLE ROLLIN' ROVER**
Both dogs lie down and roll over on command. Make sure that you space the dogs out enough to that they don't bump into one another if their rolls don't quite go according to plan.

**GROUP WAVE**
Ask all your dogs to seat in a neat row and then say goodbye to your guests with a wave. The more paws waving the merrier!

**MIX AND MATCH**
You could try something more advanced and ask each dog to perform something different at the same time. Make sure that both dogs are quite comfortable with one another's presence and that each has enough space to perform his trick safely.

**2** During separate training sessions ask your dog to "Take" the corner of his blanket in his mouth. Some dogs prefer it if you knot the corner at first. Holding fabric like this may take some getting used to so build up very gradually until he can hold on very firmly.

**3** You can now join the two tasks together. Ask him to "Take" the corner of the blanket that you hand him and then immediately ask him to lie flat on the floor. (If you've been using the cue "Bang bang" to get this move, use it now). Hopefully your dog will lie down, pulling the blanket over himself.

If he succeeds, make sure you praise him and offer a fantastic treat. Repeat this move a few times to make sure your dog understands that it brings wonderful rewards.

**THE FINALE NEEDS LOTS OF PRACTICE**
If he drops the corner of the blanket before lying flat, then go back and reinforce the take and hold part of the game again. Keep practicing over several sessions, then start to introduce your new cue before the old one; "Night night, bang bang." Gradually he will start to understand what "Night night" is indicating and you will have a fun party piece to show off. Eventually you can encourage your dog to pick up the blanket by himself before pulling it over himself. This perfects the performance.

This owner's raised foot is a cue for a group wave.

155

# COMPETITIVE GAMES

If you have a more competitive nature and enjoy pitting your dog's talents against others, there are formal canine groups that you can join. For others, these groups provide an outlet for your dog's energy and instincts. Being part of these groups should be fun and often provides a great social network with other dog owners. Choose a sport to suit your dog's physical abilities as well as your interests to maximize enjoyment for you both. I shall here briefly describe some of the options that are open to you.

**ABOVE** Flyball is a fast and furious relay game. Each dog in a team races over a set of hurdles to a box from which a ball is launched. The dog much catch it and race back to the start line where he "tags" the next team member.

**Agility** is probably one of the best known competitive canine sports. Owners have to guide their dogs (which are off-lead) around a set obstacle course involving jumps, tunnels and A-frames while incurring as few faults as possible, and in as short a time as possible. Success comes from the dog's physical ability but also his owner's dedication to the training, clarity of signals (both verbal and through body language) and their ability to keep up as they run the course! Mini-agility is also very popular, so smaller dogs need not miss out on this great sport.

**ABOVE** Dogs of every shape and size can take part in agility competitions. Fences are graded according to relative size.

**Flyball** is a high energy, precision game which involves a team of dogs that must race, one by one, over hurdles to a flyball box which the dog triggers with his paws. A ball is catapulted into the air and the dog must catch it. He then has to race back to the start with the ball where the next team member is released. The race is timed and the teams try to avoid any faults as they go.

RIGHT In disc dog competitions dogs are awarded points for catches based on the distance of the throw, with mid-air catches like this rating extra points. Contestants have 60 seconds per round.

**Frisbee, Flying Disc or Disc Dog** is a game that's ever-growing in popularity. It takes the common park game to a new level requiring speed and precision from both dog and handler. The aim is for the dog to catch and retrieve the Frisbee as many times as possible within a given time frame. Additional points are awarded for distance thrown and for more complex catch maneuvers.

**Obedience** is a highly controlled canine activity that aims for exact precision of movement and perfect responses to the owner's commands. Lots of time and dedication is required to reach the high standards and excellent distance control required.

**Heelwork to Music or Canine Freestyle** groups involve a carefully coordinated owner-dog team that perform a choreographed routine in time to their chosen soundtrack. Precision and complex movements which are in time and express the mood of the music will earn points. Heelwork to music focuses on the owner-dog pair moving together while freestyle allows more independent movement in order to express the spirit of the music.

**Earthdog Trials** If your terrier isn't cut out for the more formal canine sports, he may enjoy taking part in earthdog trials. This sport allows terriers and dachshunds to follow their instincts in a competitive arena without any small animals getting hurt in the process. The aims of these groups are to maintain and preserve the terrier's natural abilities. The trials involve man-made underground tunnels that the dogs must negotiate, while scenting a rat, the quarry.

LEFT In Canine Freestyle competitors often dress up in costume to match the choice of music to which they and their dog dance in unison.

ABOVE Lure coursing tries to stimulate the hound's natural instincts for coursing. An artificial lure is tied to a line that is pulled around an irregular course by an electric motor.

**Lure Coursing** This sport is an option for owners with sighthounds. It aims to provide an outlet for your dog's natural instincts in a safe environment without harming any small animal.

**Dock Diving or Splash Dogs** Dogs that adore water will love this fun and energetic canine sport. The competition involves the dogs diving from a ramp into the water in order to retrieve a toy. This sport is more common in warmer areas but is growing in popularity all the time, probably due to the amount of fun the dogs and owners have while taking part.

**Tracking** There are different levels of this activity to suit most dogs with a keen nose. Some groups train for tracking trials which involve the dogs following a deliberately laid trail to find the "lost" person. For those of you with plenty of time to dedicate to it, formal Search And Rescue (SAR) training is also an option. Dogs will have to participate in lots of training runs to prepare them for the real-life searches that you may be called out to attend.

**CaniX** is a sport that includes all breeds and all fitness levels. If you enjoy running then this is an ideal sport for you to join. Regular races occur throughout the year and include everyone from age 11 upwards. Aim for the 1.6 mile (2.5 km) runs and work your way up. All breeds are welcomed as long as they are fit and healthy enough to run.

**Sledding** is often thought to be only suited for Siberian Huskies or Alaskan Malamutes. However, nowadays there are many breeds other than the native northern breeds taking part. This sport is also called "Mushing" and involves physically fit and strong dogs

LEFT Splash dogs are judged according to the distance or height they achieve when jumping from a dock into a body of water.

*ABOVE Dog sled teams need to be very carefully balanced as a unit, and teams are put together with great care.*

pulling a sled with their owner in tow. Don't worry if you don't live in a snowy area as sled-dog teams can also pull wheeled sledges across grass.

**Field Trials** The purpose of this sport is to perfect the abilities of gundog breeds in an activity that closely resembles their intended purpose. The details of what your dog will be required to do will depend on what kind of gundog you own. It is best to join your local field trials group, or observe them at a Game Fair to see if this would suit you.

**Herding Trials** It may surprise you to know that herding dogs don't actually all do the same job. British herders like the Border Collie are primed to run out and round up sheep spread across a hillside. They have to be able to work at a great

distance from their owner to get the job done. Breeds that were used to tend livestock living on the mountains of the continent had to work primarily as stock protectors since the livestock were kept on smaller spaces and the greatest risk was from predators. Depending on your dog's natural history, you can find a herding group to suit you.

**Rally-Obedience** This new fun sport involves the owner and dog working their way around a course designed by the judges. At each station they find an obedience action which must be completed. The handler must ask the dog to perform this action without using food or toys.

*ABOVE A sheepdog (or herding) trial is a competitive sport in which a herding dog will move sheep around a field, through gates and into enclosures as directed by its handler.*

# ACKNOWLEDGMENTS

Thanks to all the people who've been involved in the production and development of this book at all stages. Thank you to my colleagues who suggested a few of their favorite games ideas for inclusion. A big thank you to animal handler, Sue Ottmann, for assisting me so well at the photoshoots and for helping to gather together such lovely owners and dogs. I'd also like to thank my husband Ross for once again supporting me and tolerating my late night typing and express my gratitude to Ruth Nicholls who gave up her time to proof-read my text and offer her useful comments.

I'm extremely grateful to all the owners who gave their time and lent us their well-behaved dogs for photography: Ade Akinlaja, Kathryn Baker, Samantha Clark, Jill and Les Craddock, Mrs Crome, Maggie Foster, Gill Hutton, Sheila Gordon, Heather Leach, Jean and Kate Manson, Prashant Navaratnarajah, Sheila Odi, Tania and Graham O'Donnell, Naomi Ollington, Sue Ottmann, Jon Pick, Mari Roberts, Daniella Sines, Jim Stevenson, Liz Stott, Sarah Treagus, Marie Usher, Josh Whitehead, Christine Wilkey, Nicola Wilkinson. It was lovely working with you.

# PICTURE CREDITS

Unless otherwise credited here, all the photographs in the book were taken for, and are the copyright of, Interpet Publishing.

**Jane Burton, Warren Photographic:** 54 bottom left, 108 (German Shepherd Dog), 109 (Spinone).

**Crestock.com**
Yuri Arcurs: 15 top. godfer: 15 bottom right.

**Dreamstime.com**
Arekdadej: 50 centre (dog). Colleen Crowley: 44 top right. EastWest Imaging: 47 bottom left. Kessu1: 45 bottom centre. Erik Lam: 44 centre left. Ljupco: 36 top. Nivi: 41 top. Raycan: 47 centre (dog). Damian Stoszko: 38 bottom left. Marzanna Syncerz: 24 top. Simone van den Berg: 44 bottom centre. Anke Van Wyk: 22 bottom left.

**fotolia.com**
Yuri Arcurs: 12 top left. Bertys30: 20 top. Biglama: 46 top right. CallallooAlexis: 5 bottom, 13 bottom right. Carnivore: 18 bottom left. Clearviewstock: 159 bottom right. Crimson: 158 top left. Dagel: 49 centre right. Dngood: 46 top left. EastWest Imaging: 39 bottom left. Pontus Edenberg: 158 bottom. Harvey Hudson: 20 bottom. Eric Isselée: 14 bottom right. Valeriy Kirsanov: 11 top left. Jesse Kunerth: 19 top. Monkey Business: 21 bottom. Lee O'Dell: 106-7 centre. Mikko Pitkänen: 5 centre left, 30 centre. Joe Pitz: 30 top left. Racerunner: 46 centre. Shevs: 14 bottom left. Sima: 19 bottom right. Sparkmom: 22 top. Alexey Stiop: 24 centre. Antonio Vitale: 49 top left. Ivonne Wierink: 13 top left. Sandra Zuerlein: 11 top right.

**iStockphoto.com**
Brian Asmussen: 27 top right. Thomas Bedenk: 35 bottom. Daniel Bobrowsky: 48 top. Carrie Bottomley: 5 bottom right, 29 bottom right. Dan Brandenburg: 143. Patty Colabuono: 36 bottom left. Cpaquin: 29 centre (box). Jaimie Duplass: 103 bottom left. Adam Edwards: 10 bottom. Donald Erickson: 28 top left, 29 centre left (loose treats). Kirk Geisler: 17 top. Eric Hull: 157 top. Iofoto: 53 bottom. Eric Isselée: 52 top. Fenne Kustermans: 51 bottom. Li Kim Goh: 29 top left. Drew Hadley: 26 left. Sirko Hartmann: 17 bottom. Stephanie Horrocks: 11 bottom right. Henk Jelsma: 18 top left. Peter Kim: 25 top. Erik Lam: 13 top right, 37 top. Joris Louwes: 45 top. Joanna Pecha: 26 right. Benoit Rousseau: 159 top left. Yulia Saponova: 51 top right. Rui Saraiva: 140 (pipe). Boris Shapiro: 18 centre left. Lisa Svara: 12 bottom. Lisa Kyle Young: 156 top right.

**Kruuse UK Ltd:** Back cover bottom centre, 71 centre (Buster bone and cube).

**Shutterstock.com**
Hagit Berkovich: 46 bottom left. JoLin: 156 bottom left. Vladislav Lebedinski:16. Iztok Nok: 106-7 top (dog). Simone van den Berg: Front cover top left, 31 bottom centre. Elliot Westacott: 36 bottom right, 50 top left.